GW01458885

ATHEN

TRAVEL GUIDE

2025

Your Essential Travel Companion For Having a Memorable Time and Enjoying the Amazing Beauty of this place.

Albert W. Carey

Table of contents

IMPORTANT NOTE
BEFORE READING

This Athens travel guide has been meticulously curated to provide the most up-to-date and comprehensive information to enhance your travel experience. However, you will notice the absence of maps and pictures throughout this guide. This decision was made for several important reasons.

The geographical landscapes, transportation networks, and tourist infrastructures are constantly evolving. Printed maps can quickly become outdated, leading to potential inaccuracies and confusion.

We encourage travelers to use real-time digital mapping services and GPS tools, which offer the most current and precise navigational information. Digital tools also allow for dynamic updates, ensuring you always have the latest information at your fingertips.

Travel is an inherently personal experience, and pictures can limit the imagination and subjective interpretation of the destinations. By not including pictures, we aim to inspire you to visualize and discover the beauty and uniqueness of each location through your own lens, fostering a more immersive and individual experience.

This approach encourages you to engage more deeply with the environment, creating memories based on personal encounters rather than preconceived images.

Excluding maps and pictures allows us to focus on providing richer and more detailed textual content. This ensures that you have access to essential insights, tips, and recommendations that are crucial for planning and enjoying your trip. Our goal is to equip you with the knowledge and context needed to make informed decisions and to enhance your travel experience.

We trust that this approach will enhance your journey, encouraging exploration and personal discovery. Thank you for your understanding and happy travels!

Introduction to Athens

Welcome to Athens: The Cradle of Western Civilization

Welcome to Athens, a city where ancient history and modern vibrancy merge seamlessly to create an unparalleled travel experience. As the birthplace of democracy, philosophy, and drama, Athens stands as a living monument to the achievements of the ancient world.

Yet, beyond its historical significance, Athens is a dynamic metropolis, bustling with life, culture, and endless possibilities for discovery.

Upon arriving in Athens, the first thing you'll notice is the awe-inspiring presence of the Acropolis, perched majestically atop a rocky hill in the heart of the city. This ancient citadel, crowned by the Parthenon, is more than just an archaeological wonder; it's a symbol of the enduring spirit of Athens.

As you wander its grounds, you'll be transported back to the golden age of Greece, where great minds like Socrates and Plato walked the same paths. The panoramic views from the Acropolis over the sprawling cityscape below will leave you breathless, providing a stunning introduction to the vast contrasts that define Athens.

But Athens is much more than just its ancient ruins. It's a city of vibrant neighborhoods, each with its own unique character and charm. Plaka, known as the "Neighborhood of the Gods," is a labyrinth of narrow streets lined with neoclassical buildings, where you can lose yourself in the magic of old Athens.

Here, the aroma of fresh souvlaki mingles with the scent of blooming bougainvillea, while the sounds of traditional Greek music spill out from tavernas that have been serving locals and visitors alike for generations.

Venture into the Monastiraki district, and you'll find yourself at the crossroads of history and contemporary life. This bustling area is famous for its flea markets, where you can browse everything from antique treasures to modern-day crafts.

Just around the corner, the Psiri neighborhood pulses with energy as Athens' creative heart, home to street art, cutting-edge galleries, and some of the best nightlife in the city. Whether you're in the mood for a quiet drink in a hidden bar or an all-night dance party, Psiri delivers.

As you explore Athens, you'll discover that the city is not just a destination, but an experience that engages all the senses. The culinary scene is a perfect reflection of this, blending traditional flavors with modern innovation. Enjoy a leisurely meal of mezedes (small plates) at a local taverna, where each dish tells a story of Greece's rich agricultural heritage.

Don't miss the chance to savor fresh seafood at a seaside restaurant in Piraeus or try a modern twist on classic dishes at one of the city's many contemporary eateries. Athens' food scene is a celebration of its past and present, offering something to satisfy every palate.

For those who seek culture, Athens is a treasure trove. The city's museums are among the best in the world, with the Acropolis Museum and the National Archaeological Museum offering deep dives into Greece's ancient past.

Yet, Athens also embraces the contemporary, with institutions like the Stavros Niarchos Foundation Cultural Center showcasing modern art, music, and performance.

Beyond the cultural landmarks, Athens is a city that invites exploration. Wander through the leafy National Garden, relax in a café in the hip Kolonaki district, or take a day trip to the nearby Saronic Islands for a taste of the Aegean's beauty.

Why Visit Athens?

Athens, a city where the ancient and the contemporary coexist in perfect harmony, offers a unique travel experience that combines the rich legacy of the past with the vibrant energy of the present.

Here's why visiting Athens is an opportunity to explore a city where timeless culture meets modernity:

Historical Wonders in a Modern Landscape

Athens is home to some of the world's most iconic historical landmarks, including the Acropolis, the Parthenon, and the Temple of Olympian Zeus. These ancient marvels are set against the backdrop of a bustling, modern metropolis, creating a striking contrast that is uniquely Athenian.

As you explore the city, you'll find ancient ruins seamlessly integrated into everyday life, with archaeological sites nestled between contemporary buildings and modern art installations.

A Thriving Contemporary Culture

While Athens is steeped in history, it is also a hub of contemporary culture. The city boasts a dynamic arts scene, with everything from cutting-edge galleries in neighborhoods like Psiri and Metaxourgeio to the world-class Stavros Niarchos Foundation Cultural Center, which hosts a variety of modern performances and exhibitions.

Athens is also known for its vibrant street art, which transforms the city's walls into canvases that reflect its social and political pulse.

Culinary Fusion

Athens offers a culinary experience that bridges the gap between tradition and innovation. In this city, you can savor classic Greek dishes like moussaka, fresh seafood, and baklava in traditional tavernas that have been serving locals for generations.

At the same time, Athens' culinary scene is evolving, with innovative chefs reinterpreting Greek cuisine in contemporary restaurants. This fusion of old and new flavors makes dining in Athens an adventure in itself.

Modern Infrastructure with Ancient Roots

Athens has evolved into a modern city with advanced infrastructure, including an efficient metro system that not only connects different parts of the city but also serves as a showcase for the city's archaeological treasures.

As you travel through the city, you'll encounter a blend of sleek, modern architecture and historical landmarks, reflecting Athens' ability to honor its past while embracing the future.

Vibrant Nightlife and Social Scene

The nightlife in Athens is as diverse as the city itself, offering something for every taste. From rooftop bars with stunning views of the Acropolis to lively clubs and traditional bouzouki music venues, Athens comes alive after dark.

The city's neighborhoods each have their own unique vibe, whether it's the trendy bars of Gazi or the chic cafes of Kolonaki. This blend of old-world charm and modern energy makes Athens' social scene one of the most exciting in Europe.

Cultural Events and Festivals

Athens is a city that celebrates both its ancient traditions and its modern creativity. Throughout the year, the city hosts numerous festivals and cultural events that highlight this blend.

The Athens Epidaurus Festival, for example, features performances of ancient Greek drama in historical venues alongside contemporary theatre, music, and dance. These events offer a chance to experience the city's rich cultural heritage while engaging with its modern artistic expression.

A Gateway to the Greek Islands

While Athens itself is a treasure trove of experiences, it also serves as the gateway to the stunning Greek islands. From the bustling port of Piraeus, you can easily catch a ferry to the Saronic Islands or the Cyclades, where you can explore picturesque beaches, traditional villages, and crystal-clear waters.

The proximity of these islands adds an extra dimension to your visit, allowing you to combine the cultural richness of Athens with the natural beauty of the Aegean.

Athens at a Glance: Quick Facts

Athens, the capital of Greece, is a city where the echoes of the ancient world resonate in every corner, blending seamlessly with the rhythm of modern life. This city, one of the oldest in the world, is a treasure trove of history, culture, and vibrant energy.

Are you're a history buff, a culture enthusiast, or a traveler looking for an unforgettable experience, Athens offers something for everyone.

Location and Geography

Athens is nestled in the Attica region, in the southern part of Greece, near the Aegean Sea. Surrounded by mountains on three sides and opening to the sea on the fourth, the city enjoys a strategic location that has historically made it a center of commerce and culture.

The city's landscape is a fascinating mix of ancient ruins, modern buildings, and green spaces, all set against the backdrop of the Acropolis, the city's most iconic landmark.

Population and Language

With a population of approximately 3.1 million people in the metropolitan area, Athens is the largest city in Greece and one of Europe's oldest continuously inhabited cities.

The official language is Greek, but English is widely spoken, especially in areas frequented by tourists, making it easy for visitors to communicate and navigate the city.

Currency and Time Zone

Athens, like the rest of Greece, uses the Euro (€) as its currency. Visitors will find that most establishments, from restaurants to shops, accept major credit cards, but it's always handy to have some cash for smaller transactions.

The city operates on Eastern European Time (EET), which is UTC+2, and during daylight saving time, it shifts to Eastern European Summer Time (EEST), UTC+3.

Climate

Athens enjoys a Mediterranean climate, characterized by hot, dry summers and mild, wet winters. Summer temperatures often soar above 30°C (86°F), sometimes reaching as high as 40°C (104°F) during heatwaves, making it ideal for sun-seekers.

Winters are mild, with temperatures ranging from 10-15°C (50-59°F), perfect for exploring the city without the summer crowds. The pleasant climate makes Athens a year-round destination, whether you're looking to soak up the sun or delve into the city's indoor attractions during cooler months.

Historical Significance

Athens is widely regarded as the "Cradle of Western Civilization" and the birthplace of democracy. The city's recorded history spans over 3,400 years, and its influence on culture, philosophy, and politics is immeasurable.

Landmarks such as the Acropolis, the Parthenon, and the Ancient Agora are not just tourist sites but symbols of the ideas and values that have shaped the modern world. Exploring Athens is like taking a journey through time, where every stone tells a story of its glorious past.

Iconic Landmarks

The Acropolis, with its crowning glory, the Parthenon, dominates the Athenian skyline and is a must-visit for anyone coming to the city. The Ancient Agora, once the heart of public life in Athens, and the Temple of Olympian Zeus, a colossal ruined temple, are also key attractions that offer glimpses into the city's illustrious history.

These sites are not just remnants of the past but living monuments that continue to inspire awe and admiration.

Modern Attractions

Athens is not just about its ancient heritage; it is also a vibrant, modern metropolis. The National Archaeological Museum houses one of the world's richest collections of Greek antiquities, while the Acropolis Museum, with its state-of-the-art design, showcases artifacts from the Acropolis in a stunning setting.

The Stavros Niarchos Foundation Cultural Center is a symbol of modern Athens, offering a space for contemporary art, performances, and public gatherings.

Transportation

Getting around Athens is convenient and efficient. The city boasts a modern metro system that not only connects different neighborhoods but also features archaeological exhibits in some stations.

Buses and trolleys provide extensive coverage throughout the city, while the tram connects central Athens to the coastal areas, offering a scenic route to the Athenian Riviera. Taxis are plentiful and affordable, and the Piraeus Port serves as the main gateway to the Greek islands, making island-hopping easy.

Culinary Scene

Athens is a gastronomic delight, offering a mix of traditional Greek dishes and contemporary cuisine. From classic dishes like moussaka, souvlaki, and baklava in traditional tavernas to innovative dining experiences in modern restaurants, the city's culinary scene is diverse and vibrant.

Street food, such as gyros and koulouri (a sesame-covered bread ring), is also popular and provides a quick, delicious bite on the go.

Shopping and Nightlife

Shopping in Athens is an experience in itself. The Monastiraki Flea Market is a bustling hub where you can find everything from antiques to souvenirs, while Ermou Street and Kolonaki offer high-end fashion and designer boutiques.

Athens' nightlife is legendary, with options ranging from traditional music venues to chic bars and nightclubs. Neighborhoods like Psiri, Gazi, and Kolonaki come alive after dark, offering something for every taste.

Events and Festivals

Athens hosts a variety of cultural events and festivals throughout the year. The Athens Epidaurus Festival is a highlight, featuring performances in ancient theatres.

The Athens Marathon, following the historic route from Marathon to Athens, attracts runners from around the world. Religious celebrations like Easter and Christmas are marked with traditional events, processions, and special foods, offering a deep dive into Greek culture.

Emergency Information

For any emergencies, the key numbers to remember are: Police - 100, Ambulance - 166, and Fire Brigade - 199. These services are efficient and responsive, ensuring that help is always available when needed.

Best Time To Visit Athens

Choosing the best time to visit Athens depends on what you want to experience in this vibrant city. Athens has something to offer year-round, but the seasons can significantly influence your experience.

Here's a breakdown of what each season brings, helping you decide the perfect time to explore the Greek capital.

Spring (March to May)

Best For: Sightseeing, cultural events, pleasant weather

Spring is arguably the best time to visit Athens. The weather is mild, with temperatures ranging from 15°C to 25°C (59°F to 77°F), making it perfect for exploring the city's historical sites, like the Acropolis, without the intense heat of summer. The city's parks and gardens are in full bloom, adding a splash of color to your visit.

During spring, the tourist crowds are smaller compared to the peak summer months, allowing you to enjoy attractions without long lines. The spring is also a time for cultural events and festivals, such as the Athens Epidaurus Festival, which begins in late May and features theater performances in ancient venues.

Summer (June to August)

Best For: Beach excursions, nightlife, festivals

Summer in Athens is hot and bustling with activity. Daytime temperatures can soar above 30°C (86°F), and occasionally reach up to 40°C (104°F) during heatwaves. However, the city's vibrant atmosphere, longer days, and lively nightlife make summer an exciting time to visit.

Athens' proximity to the coast means that you can easily escape the heat by heading to the nearby beaches along the Athenian Riviera. The city also hosts numerous summer events, including open-air concerts, outdoor cinema screenings, and traditional Greek festivals. However, summer is the peak tourist season, so expect larger crowds at popular sites like the Acropolis and higher prices for accommodation.

Autumn (September to November)

Best For: Sightseeing, pleasant weather, fewer crowds

Autumn is another excellent time to visit Athens. The weather remains warm in September, with temperatures gradually cooling down to around 15°C to 20°C (59°F to 68°F) by November. The summer crowds have dispersed, making it easier to explore the city's attractions and enjoy its rich history.

The mild autumn weather is ideal for outdoor activities, such as walking tours, hiking on nearby Mount Lycabettus, or exploring the Athenian Riviera's beaches. Cultural events and festivals continue into the autumn months, including the Athens International Film Festival and various art exhibitions.

Winter (December to February)

Best For: Budget travel, museums, Christmas festivities

Winter in Athens is mild compared to other European cities, with temperatures averaging between 10°C and 15°C (50°F to 59°F). While it can be cooler and rainier, winter is the off-peak season, which means fewer tourists, lower hotel prices, and shorter lines at major attractions.

Winter is a great time to explore Athens' indoor attractions, such as its world-class museums like the National Archaeological Museum and the Acropolis Museum. The city also comes alive with festive decorations and events during the Christmas season, including Christmas markets and traditional celebrations.

Chapter One
Planning Your Trip to Athens

Visa and Entry Requirements

Planning a trip to Athens, the historic capital of Greece, is an exciting endeavor. However, before you immerse yourself in the city's rich culture and explore its ancient ruins, it's essential to understand the visa and entry requirements for Greece, as these will determine how smoothly your travel preparations go.

Visa Requirements for EU/EEA Citizens

If you are a citizen of the European Union (EU) or the European Economic Area (EEA), you're in luck: you do not need a visa to enter Greece.

Thanks to the freedom of movement within the EU/EEA, citizens of these countries can travel, live, and work in Greece without any visa restrictions. You'll only need a valid passport or a national identity card to enter the country.

Visa Requirements for Non-EU/EEA Citizens

For travelers from outside the EU/EEA, the visa requirements for Greece will vary depending on your nationality. Greece is a member of the Schengen Area, a group of 27 European countries that have abolished passport control at their mutual borders.

This means that if you are from a country that is part of the Schengen Agreement, you can travel to Greece and other

Schengen countries for up to 90 days within a 180-day period without a visa.

Schengen Visa

If your country is not part of the Schengen Agreement, you will need to apply for a Schengen visa before you can enter Greece. A Schengen visa allows you to travel to any of the 27 Schengen countries for tourism, business, or family visits for up to 90 days within a 180-day period.

Here's a step-by-step guide to applying for a Schengen visa for Greece:

Determine if you need a visa: Check whether your country is part of the Schengen Agreement or if you need a visa to enter Greece.

Gather the required documents: These typically include a completed visa application form, a valid passport (with at least two blank pages and valid for at least three months beyond your intended stay), passport-sized photos, travel insurance, proof of accommodation, and proof of financial means.

You may also need to provide a detailed travel itinerary and a cover letter explaining the purpose of your visit.

Schedule an appointment: You'll need to schedule an appointment at the nearest Greek consulate or embassy to submit your application and biometric data (fingerprints and photo).

Attend the appointment: Bring all your documents to the appointment. You may be asked questions about your travel plans, so be prepared to provide detailed answers.

Pay the visa fee: The standard fee for a Schengen visa is €80 for adults and €40 for children aged 6-12. Children under 6 years old are exempt from the fee. The fee is non-refundable, even if your visa application is denied.

Wait for the decision: Processing times for Schengen visas vary, but you should generally allow at least 15 days from the date of your appointment.

During peak travel seasons, processing times may be longer, so it's advisable to apply well in advance of your intended travel dates.

Receive your visa: If your application is approved, your visa will be affixed to your passport. It will indicate the dates you are allowed to enter and stay in the Schengen Area.

Entry Requirements Upon Arrival in Athens

Upon arriving in Athens, all travelers must pass through immigration control. Here's what you can expect:

Passport Control: At passport control, you will need to present your passport. EU/EEA citizens can use the EU lanes for quicker processing, while non-EU/EEA travelers will need to go through the standard lanes.

Visa Check: If you require a visa to enter Greece, the immigration officer will check to ensure that your visa is valid for entry.

They may also ask questions about your stay in Greece, such as the purpose of your visit, where you will be staying, and your return or onward travel plans.

Entry Stamp: If everything is in order, the immigration officer will stamp your passport, indicating the date of your entry. This is particularly important for non-EU/EEA travelers, as it marks the beginning of your 90-day allowance within the Schengen Area.

Visa Extensions and Overstaying

If you wish to stay in Greece for longer than 90 days within a 180-day period, you will need to apply for a visa extension or a different type of visa, depending on the purpose of your stay.

Overstaying your visa or permitted stay period can result in fines, deportation, and future entry bans, so it's crucial to adhere to the terms of your visa.

Visa Exemptions and Special Cases

Certain travelers may be exempt from visa requirements or qualify for special arrangements. For example, holders of diplomatic passports from some countries may not require a visa, and travelers with a valid residence permit or long-term visa from another Schengen country may also be exempt from obtaining a separate visa for Greece.

Always check with the Greek consulate or embassy in your country to verify the specific requirements that apply to you.

Flights and How to Get to Athens

Athens, the vibrant capital of Greece, is well-connected to the rest of the world through a variety of transportation options. Whether you're flying in from another country or traveling from elsewhere in Greece.

Flights to Athens

Eleftherios Venizelos Airport (ATH)

The primary gateway to Athens is Eleftherios Venizelos International Airport (ATH), located about 20 kilometers (12 miles) east of the city center. It is Greece's busiest airport and one of the main hubs for international and domestic flights.

The airport offers numerous services and facilities, including restaurants, shops, car rental desks, and currency exchange.

International Flights

Athens is well-served by a wide range of airlines offering direct flights from major cities around the world. Key airlines that frequently operate flights to Athens include:

European Carriers: Lufthansa, British Airways, Air France, KLM, and others provide regular flights from major European cities like London, Paris, Frankfurt, and Amsterdam.

Middle Eastern Carriers: Emirates, Qatar Airways, and Etihad offer flights from cities such as Dubai, Doha, and Abu Dhabi.

North American Carriers: Direct flights are available from New York (JFK) with airlines such as Delta Air Lines and American Airlines, and from Toronto with Air Canada.

Asian Carriers: Airlines like Turkish Airlines and Singapore Airlines offer connecting flights from various Asian cities.

Domestic Flights

For those traveling within Greece, Athens is a major domestic flight hub. Most regional airports in Greece, including those on popular islands like Crete, Rhodes, and Santorini, have regular flights to Athens.

Airlines such as Aegean Airlines and Olympic Air offer frequent services between Athens and other Greek cities and islands.

Getting from the Airport to Athens

Upon arriving at Eleftherios Venizelos Airport, you have several options to get to the city center:

Metro: The Airport Metro Line (Line 3) connects the airport to central Athens, including major stations like Syntagma and Monastiraki. The journey takes about 40 minutes and trains run every 30 minutes.

Bus: Several bus lines operate between the airport and various parts of Athens. The X95 bus, for example, provides a direct route to Syntagma Square, while other buses connect the airport to neighborhoods and suburbs around the city.

Taxi: Taxis are readily available at the airport's taxi stand. The ride to the city center takes approximately 30-40 minutes, depending on traffic, and costs around €38-€54, with a higher rate applying during nighttime hours.

Car Rental: If you prefer to drive yourself, several car rental agencies have desks at the airport. Renting a car can be a convenient option if you plan to explore Athens and its surroundings or travel further afield.

Train and Bus Services from Other Greek Cities

Train: If you're traveling from other parts of Greece, such as Thessaloniki or Patras, you can take a train to Athens. The main train station in Athens is Larissa Station, located in the central part of the city. Trains from Thessaloniki typically take about 4-5 hours.

Bus: KTEL, Greece's intercity bus service, operates routes from various cities and towns to Athens. Buses arrive at the KTEL Bus Station, located in the Kifissos area of Athens, which is connected to the city center by public transport and taxis.

Ferries and Cruises

Athens is also a major port for ferries and cruise ships traveling to and from the Greek islands and other Mediterranean destinations.

The Port of Piraeus, located about 12 kilometers (7 miles) from central Athens, is the primary port serving the city. It's well-connected to Athens by metro, bus, and taxi.

Ferries: Ferries from Piraeus connect Athens with popular islands such as Santorini, Mykonos, and Crete. The journey times vary depending on the destination and type of ferry (high-speed or conventional).

Cruise Ships: Athens is a common stop on Mediterranean cruise itineraries. Cruise ships dock at the Port of Piraeus, where you can easily reach Athens by public transport or taxi.

Travel Tips

Book in Advance: For the best prices and availability, especially during peak travel seasons, it's advisable to book your flights, accommodation, and any necessary transport in advance.

Check Entry Requirements: Ensure you have the correct visa and travel documents before your departure. Verify entry requirements for Greece and any potential travel restrictions or advisories.

Arrive Early: Arrive at the airport well in advance of your flight to allow time for check-in, security screening, and potential delays.

With its well-connected transportation network, reaching Athens is relatively straightforward, whether you're arriving by air, land, or sea.

Once you arrive, you'll find a city rich in history, culture, and modern amenities, ready to offer you an unforgettable travel experience.

Travel Insurance and Health Precautions

Traveling to Athens, Greece, is an exciting opportunity to explore a city rich in history, culture, and modern attractions. To ensure your trip goes smoothly, it's essential to consider travel insurance and health precautions.

Travel Insurance

Why You Need Travel Insurance

Travel insurance provides essential coverage for unexpected events that may occur before or during your trip. It helps protect against financial losses due to various issues, such as trip cancellations, medical emergencies, lost luggage, and more.

While it's not a legal requirement, having travel insurance can offer peace of mind and financial protection.

Types of Coverage

Medical Insurance: This is crucial for covering medical expenses if you fall ill or get injured while traveling. Greece has a high standard of healthcare, but medical costs can be expensive for non-EU travelers.

Ensure your policy includes coverage for hospitalization, doctor visits, emergency evacuation, and repatriation.

Trip Cancellation and Interruption: This coverage reimburses you for non-refundable expenses if you need to cancel or cut short your trip due to unforeseen circumstances like illness, injury, or family emergencies.

Baggage and Personal Belongings: Protects against loss, theft, or damage to your luggage and personal items. This can be especially useful if you have valuable belongings or are traveling with essential equipment.

Travel Delay: Provides compensation for expenses incurred due to delays, such as accommodation and meals, if your flight is canceled or delayed.

Personal Liability: Covers legal costs and compensation if you're found liable for causing injury or damage to others.

How to Choose Travel Insurance

Compare Policies: Different insurers offer varying levels of coverage. Compare policies to ensure they meet your needs, especially regarding medical coverage and any specific activities you plan to undertake.

Check Exclusions: Review the policy details to understand what is and isn't covered. Common exclusions might include pre-existing conditions or certain high-risk activities.

Purchase Early: Buy travel insurance as soon as you book your trip. This ensures you're covered for any cancellations or disruptions that occur before your departure.

Health Precautions

Vaccinations and Health Requirements

Greece does not have specific vaccination requirements for travelers, but it's advisable to be up-to-date on routine vaccinations such as:

Routine Vaccinations: Ensure you're up-to-date on routine vaccinations such as measles, mumps, rubella (MMR), diphtheria-tetanus-pertussis (DTP), and polio.

Hepatitis A and B: Hepatitis A is recommended for most travelers, especially if you plan to visit rural areas or eat street food. Hepatitis B vaccination is advised for travelers who might have close contact with locals or require medical treatment.

Typhoid: This vaccine is recommended if you plan to visit rural areas or have concerns about food and water safety.

Health and Safety Tips

Healthcare Services: Athens has excellent healthcare facilities, including public hospitals and private clinics. If you need medical attention, hospitals like the General Hospital of Athens "Evangelismos" and private clinics like Hygeia Hospital are reputable options.

Pharmacies: Pharmacies are widely available throughout Athens, and many have English-speaking staff. They can provide over-the-counter medications and health advice.

Travel Health Precautions:

Food and Water: Athens has high standards for food and water safety. However, if you have a sensitive stomach, consider drinking bottled water and avoiding street food or unpasteurized dairy products.

Sun Protection: Athens enjoys a sunny Mediterranean climate. Protect yourself from the sun by using sunscreen, wearing hats, and staying hydrated.

Emergency Numbers: Familiarize yourself with local emergency numbers. In Greece, the general emergency number is 112.

What to Pack for Your Athens Adventure

Packing for a trip to Athens, Greece, requires a balance between practicality and style, as you'll be navigating the city's rich historical sites and vibrant modern scene.

Clothing

Weather-Appropriate Attire

Spring (March to May): Light layers are ideal, including a mix of short-sleeve shirts, long-sleeve tops, a light sweater or jacket for cooler evenings, and comfortable pants or skirts. The weather is generally mild and pleasant.

Summer (June to August): Pack lightweight, breathable clothing such as shorts, sundresses, and tank tops to stay cool in the heat.

Include a wide-brimmed hat, sunglasses, and a light scarf or shawl for sun protection. The heat can be intense, so opt for moisture-wicking fabrics.

Autumn (September to November): Similar to spring, bring a mix of short and long sleeves, a light jacket for cooler temperatures, and comfortable pants. Layers are useful as temperatures can vary throughout the day.

Winter (December to February): Pack warmer clothing, including a medium-weight jacket, sweaters, long pants, and comfortable shoes. Although winters in Athens are relatively mild, temperatures can drop, particularly in the evenings.

Comfortable Footwear

Walking Shoes: Athens is a city best explored on foot, so comfortable walking shoes are essential. Opt for sturdy, supportive shoes suitable for walking on uneven surfaces.

Sandals: If visiting during the warmer months, comfortable sandals are useful for strolling through the city and along the coast.

Evening Wear

Smart Casual: For dining out or enjoying Athens' nightlife, bring a few smart casual outfits. This might include a nice pair of pants or a skirt with a stylish top, or a casual dress. Most venues are casual, but some upscale restaurants or bars might have a dress code.

Essentials

Travel Documents

Passport and Visa: Ensure your passport is valid for at least six months beyond your intended stay. Bring any required visas or travel documents.

Travel Insurance: Carry a copy of your travel insurance policy and emergency contact numbers.

Money and Cards

Currency: Greece uses the Euro (€). Carry some cash for small purchases and places that don't accept cards.

Credit/Debit Cards: Inform your bank of your travel plans to avoid issues with your cards. Most establishments in Athens accept credit or debit cards.

Health and Safety Items

Medication: Bring any prescription medications you need, along with a copy of the prescription. Pack a small first-aid kit with basics such as band-aids, pain relievers, and any over-the-counter medicines you might need.

Hand Sanitizer and Masks: While health guidelines may vary, carrying hand sanitizer and a few masks can be useful.

Electronics

Chargers and Adapters

Chargers: Bring chargers for your phone, camera, and any other electronics. It's a good idea to carry a portable power bank for on-the-go charging.

Plug Adapters: Greece uses type C and F plugs with a standard voltage of 230V and frequency of 50Hz. If your devices have different plug types or voltages, bring a universal adapter.

Camera and Accessories

Camera: Athens is a city full of photogenic spots, so a good camera or smartphone with a quality camera is essential for capturing memories.

Extra Batteries and Memory Cards: Bring extra batteries and memory cards to ensure you don't miss any photo opportunities.

Miscellaneous

Guidebooks and Maps

Travel Guide: A travel guidebook or map of Athens can be handy for navigating the city and discovering local attractions.

Language Guide: Although many Greeks speak English, a phrasebook or language app can be helpful for basic Greek phrases.

Reusable Water Bottle

Hydration: Athens can be quite hot, especially in summer, so carry a reusable water bottle to stay hydrated.

Sun Protection

Sunscreen: High-SPF sunscreen is crucial to protect your skin from the Mediterranean sun.

Sunglasses: A good pair of sunglasses will help shield your eyes from the bright sunlight.

Travel Comfort Items

Neck Pillow: If you have a long flight or bus ride, a neck pillow can make your journey more comfortable.

Reusable Shopping Bag: For convenience and to reduce plastic waste, carry a reusable bag for shopping or carrying items.

Chapter Two
Getting Around Athens

Public Transportation: Buses, Metro, and Trams

Athens, a city where ancient history meets modern vibrancy, is well-equipped with an efficient public transportation network that simplifies getting around.

Understanding the city's buses, metro, and trams will make your exploration seamless and enjoyable.

Buses

Overview

Athens boasts an extensive bus network that covers nearly every corner of the city and surrounding areas.

Buses are operated by the Athens Urban Transport Organization (OASA) and provide a crucial service for both locals and visitors.

Key Features

Coverage: Buses connect the city center with various neighborhoods, suburbs, and key destinations such as Piraeus Port and the Athens International Airport. They are also useful for reaching areas not serviced by the metro or tram lines.

Types of Buses: The network includes standard city buses, express buses, and airport buses. Express buses, designated with the letter "X" followed by a number, offer non-stop services to major destinations like the airport.

How to Use

Routes and Schedules: Bus routes and schedules are available online through the OASA website or mobile app. Bus stops are marked with signs displaying route numbers and destinations. Digital displays at some stops provide real-time updates.

Tickets: You can purchase bus tickets from kiosks, ticket machines, or directly from the driver. Tickets must be validated before boarding, and they are valid for a specified duration of travel, including transfers between buses and other forms of public transport.

Accessibility: Most buses are accessible to people with disabilities, featuring low floors and space for wheelchairs.

Tips

Peak Hours: Buses can be crowded during peak hours (8:00-9:30 AM and 6:00-7:30 PM). Plan your journey accordingly if you wish to avoid congestion.

Plan Ahead: Although buses are frequent, it's a good idea to check schedules in advance, especially for routes to less central areas.

Metro

Overview

The Athens Metro is a modern, efficient, and reliable way to travel around the city. It is operated by Attiko Metro S.A. and consists of three lines: Line 1 (Green Line), Line 2 (Red Line), and Line 3 (Blue Line).

Key Features

Coverage: The metro system connects central Athens with key districts, major attractions, and transportation hubs, including the airport and Piraeus Port. Line 3 is particularly useful for travelers as it provides a direct connection to the airport.

Stations: Metro stations are well-equipped with signage in both Greek and English, making navigation straightforward. Stations are clean, safe, and often feature historical or artistic displays.

How to Use

Tickets: Tickets can be purchased from automated machines at metro stations or at ticket booths. Validate your ticket at the designated machines before entering the platforms. Multi-ride tickets and day passes are also available for tourists.

Schedules: The metro operates from 5:30 AM to midnight on weekdays and slightly later on weekends. Trains run frequently, approximately every 3-5 minutes during peak times and every 7-10 minutes during off-peak hours.

Tips

Rush Hour: Metro trains can get crowded during rush hours, particularly on Line 1. Plan your travel outside these peak times if possible.

Safety: The metro is generally safe, but it's wise to keep an eye on your belongings, especially in crowded trains and stations.

Trams

Overview

Athens' tram network, operated by STASY, provides a scenic and leisurely way to travel around the city, particularly along the coastal areas. It complements the metro and bus networks by covering routes that extend to the seaside.

Key Features

Coverage: The tram system runs from the southern suburbs along the coastline to the city center, offering beautiful views of the Athenian Riviera. It connects areas like Glyfada and Voula with central Athens.

Tram Lines: There are several tram lines, with Line 1 (Syntagma to Voula) being one of the most popular for both locals and tourists.

How to Use

Tickets: Tram tickets can be purchased from ticket machines at tram stops or from nearby kiosks. Like with buses and the metro, validate your ticket before boarding. Tram tickets are typically valid for travel on the tram network and for transfers to other public transportation modes within the validity period.

Schedules: Trams run from approximately 5:00 AM to midnight. They operate every 10-15 minutes, depending on the line and time of day.

Tips

Scenic Routes: Take advantage of the tram's coastal routes to enjoy scenic views of the Athenian Riviera. This is particularly enjoyable in the cooler hours of the day.

Connections: Tram lines often connect with bus and metro lines, allowing for convenient transfers. Check the network maps to plan your route effectively.

Taxis, Ride-Hailing, and Car Rentals

Navigating Athens can be convenient and flexible with a variety of transportation options, including taxis, ride-hailing services, and car rentals.

Each mode of transport offers different benefits depending on your needs and preferences.

Taxis

Overview

Taxis are a popular and accessible way to get around Athens, offering door-to-door service and flexibility. They are especially useful for travelers with heavy luggage, those arriving late at night, or when traveling to destinations not easily reached by public transport.

How to Use

Hailing a Taxi: Taxis can be hailed on the street or found at designated taxi stands throughout the city. Alternatively, you can book a taxi in advance via phone or apps.

Taxi Apps: Apps like Beat and Taxibeat allow you to book taxis easily, track your ride, and pay via the app. These services can be particularly convenient for tourists unfamiliar with the city.

Fares: Taxis use meters to calculate fares. Base rates apply, with additional charges for distance, time of day, and extra services. For example, there's a surcharge for airport transfers, luggage, and trips during nighttime hours.

Payment: Most taxis accept both cash and credit/debit cards. It's advisable to confirm the payment method with the driver before starting your trip.

Tips

Check the Meter: Always ensure the meter is running from the start of your journey to avoid disputes over fares.

Language: While many taxi drivers speak some English, having your destination written down or a map can be helpful.

Ride-Hailing Services

Overview

Ride-hailing services have become increasingly popular in Athens, providing a convenient and often cost-effective alternative to traditional taxis. These services offer features like cashless payments, fare estimates, and the ability to track your ride.

Key Services

Uber: Uber operates in Athens, offering various ride options including UberX and UberSelect. The app provides fare estimates, driver details, and real-time tracking.

Beat: Originally a local Greek service, Beat is now part of the global ride-hailing network. It operates similarly to Uber, with the added benefit of local knowledge and customer service.

How to Use

Download the App: Install the ride-hailing app of your choice on your smartphone. Create an account and set up your payment method.

Book a Ride: Input your pickup location and destination. The app will provide an estimated fare and connect you with a nearby driver.

Track Your Ride: You can monitor your driver's location and estimated arrival time through the app.

Tips

Safety: Ensure the car details and driver match those shown in the app before getting in. Share your ride details with a friend or family member for added security.

Surge Pricing: Be aware of surge pricing during peak times or high demand periods. The app will notify you of any additional charges.

Car Rentals

Overview

Renting a car offers the greatest flexibility for exploring Athens and its surrounding areas at your own pace. It's ideal for day trips to nearby destinations or if you prefer driving over relying on public transportation.

How to Rent a Car

Booking: Car rentals can be booked online through various agencies like Avis, Hertz, Enterprise, and local companies. It's often more economical to book in advance.

Pick-Up and Drop-Off: Most rental companies have offices at Athens International Airport and in central Athens. Check for convenient pick-up and drop-off locations based on your itinerary.

Requirements: To rent a car in Athens, you'll need a valid driver's license, a credit card, and be at least 21 years old. Some companies may have a minimum age requirement of 25 for certain vehicle categories.

Driving in Athens

Traffic: Athens can experience heavy traffic, especially during rush hours. Plan your routes and travel times accordingly.

Parking: Parking can be challenging in central Athens. Look for designated parking areas or garages. Pay attention to parking regulations to avoid fines.

Roads: Greek roads are generally well-maintained, but be cautious of narrow streets and frequent pedestrian areas in the city center.

Tips

Insurance: Ensure your rental includes adequate insurance coverage. Check for options like collision damage waivers (CDW) and theft protection.

Navigation: Use a GPS or navigation app to assist with directions and to avoid getting lost in the city's maze of streets.

Walking and Biking Around the City

Exploring Athens on foot or by bike offers a unique and immersive way to experience the city's vibrant atmosphere and historical landmarks.

Both walking and biking provide flexibility, allow for spontaneous discoveries, and help you connect with the city in a more personal way.

Walking Around Athens

Overview

Walking is one of the best ways to experience Athens, especially in the historic center where many of the city's key attractions are located. The city's compact layout and pedestrian-friendly areas make it ideal for exploring on foot.

Popular Walking Routes

Plaka District: Known as Athens' old neighborhood, Plaka is characterized by its narrow, winding streets, charming shops, and traditional tavernas. It's a perfect area to wander and absorb the city's historic ambiance.

Monastiraki to Syntagma: This route takes you from the bustling Monastiraki Square, home to the vibrant flea market and the Ancient Agora, to Syntagma Square, where you can view the Greek Parliament and the grand Hotel Grande Bretagne.

Acropolis and Surroundings: Walking up to the Acropolis is a must-do. Explore the surrounding area, including the Areopagus Hill for panoramic views of the city, and the Acropolis Museum which is a short walk away.

Kolonaki: A stylish neighborhood with upscale shops, cafes, and cultural spots like the Benaki Museum. The area is hilly, so comfortable walking shoes are recommended.

Tips for Walking

Comfortable Footwear: Wear comfortable shoes as you'll likely be walking on uneven surfaces and cobblestone streets.

Hydration and Sun Protection: Athens can be hot, especially in summer. Carry water, wear sunscreen, and use a hat or sunglasses to protect yourself from the sun.

Maps and Apps: Use a map or navigation app to help you find your way and discover points of interest along your route.

Safety: Athens is generally safe for pedestrians, but always stay aware of your surroundings and keep an eye on your belongings.

Biking Around Athens

Overview

Biking is an excellent way to explore Athens, allowing you to cover more ground while enjoying the city's diverse landscapes. The city has been improving its infrastructure to support cyclists, making it increasingly bike-friendly.

Bike-Friendly Areas

Athens Riviera: The coastal stretch from the city center to the southern suburbs, including Glyfada and Voula, is particularly scenic and enjoyable for cycling. The path along the coast offers stunning views and fresh sea breezes.

Pedion tou Areos: This large park in the center of Athens provides a green oasis and dedicated bike paths, perfect for a leisurely ride.

The National Garden of Athens: Located near Syntagma Square, this garden features pathways where you can enjoy a relaxed bike ride amidst lush greenery.

Bike Rentals

Bike Rental Shops: Several rental shops are available in Athens, offering various types of bikes, including city bikes, mountain bikes, and e-bikes. Shops such as "Athens by Bike" and "Bike.gr" offer rental services and guided bike tours.

Rental Process: Rental shops typically require a valid ID and a credit card for security. It's a good idea to book in advance, especially during peak tourist seasons.

Tips for Biking

Bike Lanes: While bike lanes are becoming more common, they are still limited. Be cautious and share the road with vehicles where bike lanes are not available.

Traffic Awareness: Athens traffic can be hectic. Always follow traffic rules, use hand signals for turning, and stay alert.

Safety Gear: Helmets are not always provided by rental companies, so consider bringing your own. Also, check the bike's condition before setting off.

Parking: Look for designated bike racks or parking areas. Avoid leaving your bike unattended in areas where it might be at risk of theft.

Day Trips from Athens: Tours and Excursions

Athens is a city rich in history and culture, but its location also makes it an excellent base for exploring a variety of nearby destinations.

If you're interested in ancient ruins, stunning landscapes, or charming seaside towns, there are numerous day trips that offer a change of pace from the city's hustle and bustle.

Delphi

Overview

Delphi, located about 180 kilometers (112 miles) northwest of Athens, was once considered the center of the world in ancient Greek mythology. This UNESCO World Heritage site is renowned for its ancient ruins and spectacular mountain setting.

Key Attractions

Temple of Apollo: The central site of Delphi, where the oracle of Apollo was consulted. The ruins include the Temple of Apollo, the ancient theater, and the stadium.

Delphi Archaeological Museum: Houses a vast collection of artifacts from the site, including the famous Charioteer of Delphi and various sculptures and inscriptions.

Sanctuary of Athena Pronaia: A picturesque site with remains of ancient temples and the Tholos, a circular building with distinctive columns.

Tours and Excursions

Guided Tours: Many tour operators offer guided day trips from Athens to Delphi. These typically include transportation, a guide, and entrance fees.

Self-Drive: Renting a car allows flexibility to explore Delphi at your own pace. The drive takes about 2.5 hours.

Tips

Wear Comfortable Shoes: The site involves a lot of walking on uneven terrain.

Book in Advance: Popular tours can fill up quickly, especially during peak tourist season.

Cape Sounion and the Temple of Poseidon

Overview

Cape Sounion is located about 70 kilometers (43 miles) southeast of Athens and offers breathtaking coastal views and ancient ruins. The highlight is the Temple of Poseidon, perched on a cliff overlooking the Aegean Sea.

Key Attractions

Temple of Poseidon: An ancient Greek temple dedicated to the sea god Poseidon. The site offers stunning sunset views over the Aegean Sea.

Sounion Beach: A nearby beach where you can relax and enjoy the sea after exploring the ruins.

Tours and Excursions

Sunset Tours: Many tours focus on the sunset at Cape Sounion, providing a beautiful end to the day.

Private Transfers: For a more flexible visit, consider booking a private transfer.

Tips

Check Sunset Times: If you're going for the sunset, check local times to plan your visit accordingly.

Bring a Camera: The views from Cape Sounion are spectacular, so don't forget your camera.

Corinth and the Ancient Corinth Archaeological Site

Overview

Located approximately 80 kilometers (50 miles) west of Athens, ancient Corinth was a major city in ancient Greece. The site includes well-preserved ruins and offers insights into the city's historical significance.

Key Attractions

Ancient Corinth Ruins: Includes the Temple of Apollo, the Roman Agora, and the Acrocorinth, a hilltop fortress with panoramic views.

Corinth Canal: A man-made canal connecting the Aegean and Ionian Seas, which is a marvel of engineering.

Tours and Excursions

Guided Tours: Many tours include visits to both the archaeological site and the Corinth Canal.

Self-Drive: Renting a car allows you to explore the region at your own pace.

Tips

Explore Acrocorinth: The fortress offers some of the best views of the surrounding area.

Wear Sunscreen: The site can be very sunny, so protect yourself from sun exposure.

Hydra Island

Overview

Hydra is a car-free island located about 70 kilometers (43 miles) from Athens. Known for its preserved architecture and stunning sea views, it offers a charming escape from the city.

Key Attractions

Hydra Town: Wander through narrow streets lined with traditional stone houses, boutiques, and cafes.

Beaches: Enjoy swimming and sunbathing at several small beaches around the island.

Tours and Excursions

Ferry Trips: Ferries to Hydra depart from Piraeus Port. The journey takes about 1 to 1.5 hours.

Private Boats: For a more personalized experience, consider chartering a private boat.

Tips

Comfortable Footwear: Since the island is car-free, be prepared to walk or use water taxis.

Cash: Many places on Hydra only accept cash, so bring enough for your needs.

Nafplio

Overview

Nafplio is a picturesque seaside town located about 140 kilometers (87 miles) southwest of Athens. It's known for its charming old town, historic sites, and beautiful waterfront.

Key Attractions

Palamidi Fortress: A Venetian fortress offering panoramic views of the town and the surrounding sea.

Bourtzi Castle: Located on a small island in the harbor, accessible by a short boat ride.

Syntagma Square: A lovely square surrounded by neoclassical buildings, cafes, and shops.

Tours and Excursions

Guided Tours: Day trips from Athens to Nafplio often include visits to nearby archaeological sites such as Epidaurus and Mycenae.

Self-Drive: Renting a car provides the freedom to explore Nafplio and its surroundings at your own pace.

Tips

Explore on Foot: The town's historic center is best explored on foot, with its narrow streets and charming squares.

Try Local Cuisine: Nafplio offers excellent dining options with fresh seafood and traditional Greek dishes.

Chapter Three
Top Attractions in Athens

The Acropolis

Dominating the skyline of Athens, the Acropolis is an awe-inspiring symbol of ancient Greek civilization. Perched atop a rocky outcrop, this ancient citadel is home to some of the most significant architectural and cultural treasures of classical Greece.

Among its many remarkable structures, the Parthenon stands out as a paragon of ancient Greek architecture, while the surrounding temples and monuments collectively offer a rich tapestry of history and artistry.

The Parthenon

Overview

The Parthenon, constructed between 447 and 432 BCE during the height of the Athenian Empire, is the centerpiece of the Acropolis and a masterpiece of ancient Greek architecture.

Dedicated to Athena Parthenos, the city's patron goddess, this temple epitomizes the grandeur and sophistication of classical Greece.

Architectural Significance

Design: Designed by architects Ictinus and Callicrates, the Parthenon is celebrated for its harmonious proportions and the

Doric order's simplicity. Its rectangular structure, supported by 46 columns, demonstrates an advanced understanding of geometry and aesthetics.

The building's slight curvature and entasis (slight bulging of columns) correct optical illusions and create a more visually pleasing effect.

Sculptures: The Parthenon once housed a colossal statue of Athena, crafted by the sculptor Phidias. Although the original statue has been lost, detailed descriptions and replicas illustrate its monumental scale and artistic brilliance.

The temple's friezes and metopes, also by Phidias, depict scenes from Greek mythology and history, such as the Panathenaic Procession and battles between gods and giants.

Visiting Tips

Entry: Access to the Parthenon is included with a general ticket to the Acropolis. To avoid long lines, consider purchasing tickets online or visiting early in the morning or late in the afternoon.

Photography: The site offers spectacular photographic opportunities, especially during sunrise or sunset when the light casts a golden glow over the ancient ruins.

The Erechtheion

Overview

The Erechtheion, built between 421 and 406 BCE, is an architectural marvel renowned for its unique and irregular design, which adapted to the uneven terrain of the Acropolis.

This temple was dedicated to both Athena and Poseidon and housed sacred relics and the olive tree believed to have been gifted by Athena.

Architectural Features

Design: The Erechtheion's asymmetrical design and multiple levels accommodate the natural slope of the Acropolis. The temple features a mix of Ionic and archaic elements, showcasing its adaptation to the site's topography.

Caryatids: The most famous feature of the Erechtheion is the Porch of the Caryatids, where six elegantly draped female figures replace traditional columns. These Caryatids, originally sculpted by Phidias' workshop, now stand in the Acropolis Museum, with replicas in place.

Visiting Tips

Details: Pay close attention to the intricate details of the Caryatids and the Erechtheion's innovative architectural solutions. The temple's design reflects its religious significance and the adaptation to the challenging terrain.

Access: The Erechtheion is often less crowded than the Parthenon, providing a more intimate experience of its historical and architectural significance.

The Temple of Athena Nike

Overview

The Temple of Athena Nike, built between 427 and 424 BCE, is a small but exquisitely designed Ionic temple located at the southwest corner of the Acropolis. Dedicated to Athena Nike, the goddess of victory, it symbolizes Athenian triumphs and the city's military prowess.

Architectural Features

Design: The temple is celebrated for its elegant proportions and detailed ornamentation. Its four-columned structure and frieze depict historical battle scenes, celebrating Athenian military victories.

Sculptures: The frieze of the Temple of Athena Nike portrays scenes of battles and processions, demonstrating the dynamic and intricate style of classical Greek sculpture.

Visiting Tips

Intimate Experience: The Temple of Athena Nike's smaller size allows for a close-up view of its detailed carvings and architectural elegance. Take time to appreciate the fine craftsmanship and historical context.

Views: The temple offers stunning views of the surrounding landscape, including the Athenian Agora and the city beyond.

The Odeon of Herodes Atticus

Overview

Although not a temple, the Odeon of Herodes Atticus, an ancient theater built in 161 CE by the Roman aristocrat Herodes Atticus, is an integral part of the Acropolis complex.

The theater was designed for dramatic and musical performances and remains a significant cultural venue.

Architectural Features

Design: The Odeon features a semi-circular auditorium with a capacity of around 5,000 spectators, a grand stage, and intricate marble decorations. Its design reflects Roman architectural influence while maintaining classical Greek aesthetics.

Restorations: The theater has undergone several restorations and continues to host performances, including those of the Athens Festival.

Visiting Tips

Events: Check the schedule for events or performances at the Odeon of Herodes Atticus to experience a show in this historic venue.

Acoustic Experience: The theater's exceptional acoustics allow for an immersive experience of its architectural and historical significance.

Acropolis Museum: Ancient Artifacts and Modern Exhibits

The Acropolis Museum, situated at the foot of the Acropolis in Athens, stands as a modern marvel that complements the ancient grandeur of the Acropolis itself. Designed by architect Bernard Tschumi, the museum offers an exceptional space to explore and appreciate the artistic and cultural treasures of ancient Greece.

Opened in 2009, the museum showcases a vast array of artifacts from the Acropolis and its surrounding areas, blending cutting-edge design with rich historical content.

The Museum's Architecture

Overview

The Acropolis Museum's architecture is a masterful integration of modern design with the historical context of its location. The building is constructed with transparency in mind, featuring extensive glass facades that offer views of the Acropolis and allow natural light to illuminate the exhibits.

Design Features

Transparent Design: The museum's glass floors and walls provide a visual connection to the archaeological site beneath, creating a sense of continuity between the ancient and the modern.

Elevated Walkways: The design includes elevated walkways that guide visitors through the museum's various levels and exhibitions, offering different perspectives of the artifacts and their historical context.

The Parthenon Gallery

Overview

The Parthenon Gallery is the highlight of the museum, dedicated to displaying the Parthenon's sculptures and architectural elements. Located on the top floor, this gallery is aligned with the Parthenon's orientation and showcases the temple's original sculptures in a setting that mirrors their historical placement.

Key Exhibits

The Parthenon Marbles: This gallery houses the Parthenon Marbles, including the friezes, metopes, and pedimental sculptures.

These pieces illustrate key events from Greek mythology and Athenian history, such as the Panathenaic Procession and the Gigantomachy.

Reconstruction: The gallery features a partial reconstruction of the Parthenon's frieze and metopes, allowing visitors to see how the sculptures once adorned the temple.

Visiting Tips

Viewpoints: The gallery's design provides excellent viewpoints to appreciate the intricate details of the sculptures and their historical significance.

Interactive Displays: Look for interactive displays and digital reconstructions that offer insights into the original placement and context of the Parthenon sculptures.

The Archaic Gallery

Overview

The Archaic Gallery, located on the museum's ground floor, focuses on the period before the construction of the Parthenon, showcasing artifacts from the 7th to the 5th centuries BCE.

This gallery provides a deeper understanding of the artistic evolution leading up to the Classical era.

Key Exhibits

Kouroi and Korai: The gallery displays a collection of Kouroi (statues of young men) and Korai (statues of young women), which highlight the development of Greek sculpture from rigid, stylized forms to more naturalistic representations.

Early Temples: Artifacts from early temples on the Acropolis, including offerings and sculptures, illustrate the religious practices and artistic styles of the period.

Visiting Tips

Contextual Information: Take time to read the detailed descriptions and historical context provided for each artifact, which offer insights into the early phases of Greek art and religion.

Comparison: Compare the Archaic sculptures with later Classical works to appreciate the evolution of Greek art and its impact on subsequent styles.

The Gallery of the Acropolis Slopes

Overview

This gallery features artifacts discovered on the slopes of the Acropolis, providing a broader view of the religious and social activities that took place in the vicinity of the ancient citadel.

Key Exhibits

Sanctuary Artifacts: Items from the sanctuary of Asklepios and other surrounding religious sites, including votive offerings and inscriptions, shed light on the practices and rituals of ancient Athenians.

Daily Life Objects: Objects related to daily life, such as pottery and tools, offer a glimpse into the everyday activities of ancient Athenians.

Visiting Tips

Thematic Displays: Explore the thematic displays that group artifacts according to their use and significance, enhancing your understanding of their historical context.

Educational Programs: Check for educational programs or guided tours that provide deeper insights into the artifacts and their relevance to ancient Athenian life.

Museum Facilities and Services

Overview

The Acropolis Museum offers various facilities and services to enhance the visitor experience, making it a comfortable and informative destination.

Facilities

Cafeteria and Restaurant: Enjoy Greek cuisine and refreshments at the museum's cafeteria or restaurant, which offer stunning views of the Acropolis.

Museum Shop: The shop features a range of books, replicas, and souvenirs related to the exhibits and Greek heritage.

Educational Programs: The museum provides educational programs, workshops, and lectures that delve into the history and significance of the Acropolis and its artifacts.

Visiting Tips

Plan Ahead: Check the museum's website for information on opening hours, ticket prices, and special exhibitions or events.

Accessibility: The museum is designed to be accessible to all visitors, with facilities and services catering to various needs.

The Ancient Agora: Birthplace of Democracy

The Ancient Agora of Athens is a compelling destination that offers a deep dive into the heart of classical Athenian civilization. As the cradle of democracy and a bustling center of public life, the Agora provides a window into the political, social, and cultural practices of ancient Greece.

Planning Your Visit

Address and Location

The Ancient Agora is centrally located in Athens, making it easy to reach from various parts of the city. The address is:

Ancient Agora of Athens

Adrianou 24, Athina 105 55, Greece

Opening Hours

Daily: Generally open from 8:00 AM to 8:00 PM. Extended hours might be available during peak tourist seasons. Always verify the latest hours before visiting.

Admission Fees

Standard Ticket: Includes access to the Ancient Agora and the Stoa of Attalos Museum. Ticket prices may vary, with discounts offered to students, senior citizens, and in certain off-peak periods.

Accessibility

Facilities: The site is equipped with ramps and pathways for wheelchair access. There are restrooms and refreshment options available nearby. Comfortable walking shoes are recommended due to the uneven terrain.

Key Attractions to Explore

The Stoa of Attalos

Overview

The Stoa of Attalos, originally constructed in the 2nd century BCE by King Attalos II of Pergamon, was a grand colonnaded structure used for various civic activities.

The building was meticulously reconstructed in the 1950s and now serves as the Agora Museum.

Highlights

Agora Museum: This museum houses an impressive collection of artifacts uncovered from the Agora, including sculptures, pottery, and inscriptions. It provides valuable insights into the daily life, religious practices, and administrative functions of ancient Athens.

Architectural Features: The Stoa's design features a double colonnade with Doric columns on the lower level and Ionic columns above, giving visitors a sense of the grandeur and scale of Athenian public architecture.

Visiting Tips

Guided Tours: Consider joining a guided tour to enrich your understanding of the exhibits and the historical context of the Stoa.

Photography: The museum offers excellent photo opportunities, particularly of the architectural details and the well-preserved artifacts.

The Temple of Hephaestus

Overview

The Temple of Hephaestus, also known as the Theseion, is one of the best-preserved ancient Greek temples. Dedicated to Hephaestus, the god of metalworking, and Athena Ergane, the goddess of crafts, it dates back to the 5th century BCE.

Highlights

Architectural Significance: The temple features classic Doric design with a peristyle of 6x13 columns and an elaborate interior. Its preservation provides a rare and authentic glimpse into ancient Greek religious architecture.

Historical Context: The temple's design and inscriptions offer insights into the religious practices and artistic achievements of the time.

Visiting Tips

Timing: Early mornings or late afternoons are the best times to visit to avoid crowds and enjoy a more serene experience.

Interpretive Signs: Read the interpretive signs to fully appreciate the temple's historical and cultural significance.

The Bouleuterion

Overview

The Bouleuterion was the council house where the Boule, or council of 500 citizens, convened to discuss and draft legislation. It played a crucial role in the governance of Athens.

Highlights

Architectural Layout: The Bouleuterion's rectangular plan with a semicircular seating area reflects its function as a venue for political deliberations.

Historical Insights: The ruins reveal much about the administrative and legislative processes of Athenian democracy.

Visiting Tips

Explore the Ruins: Take your time to walk through the remains and imagine the lively political debates that once took place here.

Interactive Displays: Look for information panels that provide context and background about the Bouleuterion's role in Athenian society.

The Odeon of Agrippa

Overview

The Odeon of Agrippa, constructed by the Roman general Marcus Agrippa in the 1st century BCE, was used for musical performances and public events. Though less preserved, it remains an important cultural landmark.

Highlights

Architectural Features: The Odeon's semi-circular auditorium and stage area reflect Roman influences on Greek architectural styles.

Cultural Context: The theater's role in hosting performances highlights the continued importance of public entertainment in ancient Athens.

Visiting Tips

Special Events: Check for any performances or events that might be scheduled at the Odeon, offering a unique way to experience its historical ambiance.

Photography: Capture the contrasts between the ancient structure and the modern cityscape.

Practical Tips for Your Visit

Planning Your Route

Map and Guide: Pick up a map or audio guide at the entrance to navigate the site effectively and ensure you don't miss any key attractions.

Tour Options: Consider guided tours for a more comprehensive exploration, offering insights into the historical and architectural significance of each structure.

What to Bring

Comfortable Shoes: Wear sturdy, comfortable footwear suitable for walking on uneven surfaces.

Water and Snacks: Bring water and snacks, as exploring the site can be physically demanding.

Visitor Etiquette

Respect the Site: Follow posted rules and guidelines to preserve the integrity of the site. Avoid touching the artifacts and stay on designated pathways.

The National Archaeological Museum

The National Archaeological Museum of Athens stands as one of the world's greatest repositories of ancient Greek artifacts. Located in the heart of Athens, this museum is a treasure trove of Greece's historical and cultural legacy, offering a comprehensive journey through the ancient world.

From its world-renowned collections to its architectural grandeur, the museum provides an unparalleled experience for anyone interested in Greek history and art.

Overview and Location

Address and Contact Information

National Archaeological Museum

44 Patission Street, Athens 106 82, Greece

Phone: +30 213 214 4800

Hours of Operation

Daily: Typically open from 8:00 AM to 8:00 PM. Closed on certain holidays, so it's advisable to check the museum's website for current hours before your visit.

Admission Fees

Standard Ticket: The general admission fee covers access to the museum's permanent exhibitions. Discounts are available for students, seniors, and groups. There may be an additional charge for special exhibitions.

Accessibility

Facilities: The museum is fully accessible to visitors with mobility impairments. It features ramps, elevators, and accessible restrooms. Wheelchairs are available upon request.

Key Highlights of the Museum

The Main Collections

The Prehistoric Collection

Overview

The Prehistoric Collection showcases artifacts from the Neolithic to the Bronze Age, offering insights into the early civilizations of Greece.

Highlights

Cycladic Art: Renowned for its abstract marble figurines, Cycladic art provides a glimpse into the enigmatic culture of the Cyclades islands.

Minoan Artifacts: Includes treasures from the Minoan civilization on Crete, such as intricately decorated pottery and frescoes from the palace of Knossos.

Mycenaean Artifacts: Features golden masks, jewelry, and weapons from the Mycenaean period, revealing the grandeur of this early Greek civilization.

The Sculpture Collection

Overview

The Sculpture Collection contains some of the most iconic sculptures from ancient Greece, reflecting the evolution of Greek art from the Archaic to the Classical periods.

Highlights

The Statue of Zeus or Poseidon: An imposing statue that is either Zeus or Poseidon, known for its dramatic pose and exquisite craftsmanship.

The Discobolus (Disc Thrower): A celebrated example of Classical Greek art by Myron, depicting an athlete in mid-throw.

The Kouros Statues: These statues represent idealized young men and are exemplary of Archaic Greek sculpture.

The Vase Collection

Overview

The Vase Collection presents a comprehensive overview of Greek pottery from the Geometric to the Hellenistic periods.

Highlights

Black-Figure and Red-Figure Pottery: The museum's collection includes fine examples of both styles, showcasing the evolution of Greek vase painting techniques.

Panathenaic Amphorae: Large ceremonial vases awarded as prizes during the Panathenaic Games, decorated with scenes of athletic events and religious ceremonies.

The Gold Collection

Overview

The Gold Collection features an impressive array of jewelry and other gold artifacts, reflecting the wealth and artistry of ancient Greek societies.

Highlights

The Mycenaean Treasure: Includes the famous "Mask of Agamemnon" and other gold artifacts from the royal graves of Mycenae.

Classical Jewelry: Exquisite pieces of jewelry from various Greek periods, showcasing intricate craftsmanship and design.

Practical Tips for Your Visit

Planning Your Route

Museum Map: Pick up a map at the entrance to help navigate the extensive galleries and plan your visit according to your interests.

Audio Guides: Consider renting an audio guide to gain deeper insights into the exhibits. Many guides offer detailed information about the artifacts and their historical context.

Guided Tours

Tours: Guided tours are available in multiple languages and can enhance your understanding of the museum's collections. Check the schedule and book in advance if possible.

Visitor Amenities

Café and Gift Shop: The museum features a café where you can take a break and enjoy refreshments. The gift shop offers a range of souvenirs, including replicas of famous artifacts.

Photography: Photography is generally allowed in most parts of the museum, but flash photography and tripods are usually prohibited.

Accessibility and Comfort

Comfortable Attire: Wear comfortable clothing and shoes, as you will be walking through various galleries. The museum is large, and a visit can take several hours.

Rest Areas: There are designated rest areas where you can sit and relax during your visit.

The Museum's Architecture

Overview

The National Archaeological Museum itself is a masterpiece of 19th-century architecture. Designed by the architect Ludwig Lange, the building features neoclassical elements, including grand columns, spacious halls, and beautifully decorated ceilings.

The architecture of the museum complements the significance of its collections, creating a fitting backdrop for Greece's rich historical heritage.

Mount Lycabettus: Athens' Best Panoramic View

Mount Lycabettus, rising 277 meters above sea level, offers one of the most stunning panoramic views in Athens. Often referred to as the "Lycabettus Hill," this prominent peak provides visitors with a breathtaking vista of the city, the Acropolis, and the surrounding landscape.

Overview and Location

Address and Location

Mount Lycabettus is centrally located in Athens, making it easily accessible from various parts of the city. The area around the base of the hill is also known as Lycabettus.

Base of Mount Lycabettus

Athens 114 71, Greece

Getting There

By Foot: For those who enjoy hiking, there are well-marked paths leading to the summit. The trek takes approximately 30-45 minutes depending on your pace.

By Funicular: The Lycabettus Funicular Railway offers a convenient and scenic ride to the top. The funicular station is located on Ploutarchou Street, and the journey takes about 3 minutes.

Attractions and Highlights

The Panoramic View

Overview

The summit of Mount Lycabettus provides an unrivaled panoramic view of Athens and its surroundings. On a clear day, you can see the Acropolis, the Athenian Agora, the Saronic Gulf, and even the distant mountains of the Peloponnese.

Highlights

Acropolis: Enjoy a sweeping view of the Acropolis and its ancient monuments, including the Parthenon, which looks magnificent from above.

Cityscape: Take in the sprawling cityscape of Athens, with its mix of modern and historic architecture.

Sunset Views: Mount Lycabettus is an ideal spot for watching the sunset. The changing colors of the sky as the sun sets over the city create a magical experience.

The Chapel of St. George

Overview

At the summit of Mount Lycabettus, you'll find the Chapel of St. George, a charming whitewashed building with blue domes. This small church, built in the 19th century, adds a touch of religious and historical significance to the site.

Highlights

Architecture: The chapel's traditional Greek Orthodox architecture and stunning location make it a picturesque spot for photographs.

Religious Significance: The chapel is often used for special services and ceremonies, adding a cultural dimension to your visit.

The Restaurant and Café

Overview

Near the summit, there's a restaurant and café where you can relax and enjoy refreshments while taking in the view. The dining options range from light snacks to more substantial meals.

Highlights

Outdoor Seating: Enjoy your meal or drink on the terrace, which offers uninterrupted views of Athens.

Menu: The menu features a variety of Greek and international dishes, along with coffee and desserts.

Practical Tips for Your Visit

Best Time to Visit

Morning: Early morning visits are ideal for a peaceful experience and clearer views.

Sunset: Visiting in the late afternoon or early evening allows you to experience the sunset and see the city lights come alive.

What to Bring

Comfortable Footwear: If you're hiking up the hill, wear comfortable, sturdy shoes.

Camera: Don't forget your camera or smartphone to capture the stunning views.

Accessibility

Funicular Access: The funicular provides a convenient option for those who prefer not to hike. It is accessible and offers a smooth ride to the top.

Hiking Trails: The paths to the summit can be steep and uneven. Ensure you're in good health and prepared for a moderate physical challenge.

Visitor Amenities

Rest Areas: There are seating areas around the summit where you can rest and enjoy the view.

Toilets: Restroom facilities are available at the base of the hill and near the funicular station.

History and Significance

Historical Background

Mount Lycabettus is steeped in mythology and history. According to legend, the hill was created by the goddess Athena when she threw a piece of the mountain towards the city of Athens.

Over the centuries, it has become a symbol of Athens and a popular spot for both locals and tourists.

Chapter Four
Historical and Cultural Sites

Hadrian's Library: Roman Influence in Ancient Greece

Hadrian's Library, located in the heart of Athens, is a fascinating site that offers a unique glimpse into the Roman influence on ancient Greek culture.

Established by the Roman Emperor Hadrian in 132 AD, this monumental complex was not only a center of learning and culture but also a testament to the blending of Roman and Greek architectural and cultural elements.

Overview and Location

Address and Location

Hadrian's Library is centrally situated in Athens, making it easily accessible from major landmarks and transportation hubs. The address is:

Hadrian's Library

Areopagitou 1, Athina 105 55, Greece

Getting There

By Foot: The library is within walking distance from several major attractions, including the Roman Agora and Monastiraki Square.

By Metro: The nearest metro station is Monastiraki, which is just a short walk from the site.

Opening Hours

Daily: Generally open from 8:00 AM to 8:00 PM. Extended hours may apply during peak tourist seasons. It's advisable to check current hours and possible closures before your visit.

Admission Fees

Standard Ticket: Covers access to Hadrian's Library as well as other nearby archaeological sites. Discounts may be available for students, seniors, and certain times of the year.

Accessibility

Facilities: The site is accessible to visitors with mobility impairments, with pathways and ramps designed to facilitate easy movement. Restrooms and refreshment options are available nearby.

Key Attractions to Explore

The Main Entrance and Forecourt

Overview

The main entrance of Hadrian's Library, known as the Propylon, is an impressive structure that sets the tone for the rest of the complex. The forecourt, or atrium, was a grand open space that welcomed visitors.

Highlights

Architectural Design: The Propylon features Corinthian columns and an elaborate facade, reflecting the grandeur of Roman architecture.

Historical Significance: The entrance served as a symbolic gateway to a center of learning and cultural exchange.

The Library Hall

Overview

The library hall was the central part of the complex, where scrolls and manuscripts were stored and studied. It is one of the most significant features of the site.

Highlights

Architectural Elements: The hall was originally adorned with decorative columns and marble floors. Though much of it is in ruins, the remnants provide insights into the scale and design of the library.

Historical Role: The library was a major repository of knowledge, hosting texts from both Greek and Roman traditions.

The Lecture Hall and Reading Rooms

Overview

Adjacent to the main library hall were lecture halls and reading rooms where scholars and students would gather to discuss and study various subjects.

Highlights

Design Features: The layout of the lecture halls included seating arrangements and alcoves for discussion, showcasing the Roman emphasis on education and intellectual exchange.

Cultural Impact: These spaces highlight the Roman commitment to promoting education and integrating Greek intellectual traditions.

The Baths and Complex Amenities

Overview

Hadrian's Library also included bathing facilities, reflecting the Roman practice of integrating leisure and learning. These baths were used for relaxation and socializing.

Highlights

Bathing Facilities: The ruins include the remains of an elaborate bathing complex with pools and changing rooms.

Social Function: The presence of baths underscores the Roman approach to blending public and private life, making the library a multifaceted cultural center.

The Collonaded Courtyards

Overview

The library complex featured several colonnaded courtyards, which served as communal spaces for visitors and scholars to gather.

Highlights

Architectural Beauty: The courtyards were lined with columns and adorned with decorative elements, providing a serene environment for intellectual and social activities.

Historical Context: These spaces facilitated interaction and reflection, enhancing the educational experience within the library.

Practical Tips for Your Visit

Best Time to Visit

Morning or Late Afternoon: Visiting early in the morning or late in the afternoon helps avoid the peak tourist crowds and allows for a more leisurely exploration.

What to Bring

Comfortable Shoes: Wear comfortable footwear suitable for walking and exploring uneven surfaces.

Camera: Bring a camera to capture the impressive ruins and architectural details.

Guided Tours

Tours: Consider joining a guided tour to gain deeper insights into the history and significance of Hadrian's Library. Many tours offer detailed explanations about the Roman influence on Greek culture and the architectural features of the site.

Visitor Amenities

Rest Areas: There are seating areas where you can take a break and enjoy the surroundings.

Refreshments: While there may not be food and drink facilities on site, there are cafes and shops nearby where you can purchase refreshments.

Accessibility and Comfort

Weather Considerations: Athens can be quite hot, especially in summer. Bring water, wear sunscreen, and dress appropriately for the weather.

Historical and Cultural Context

Historical Background

Hadrian's Library was constructed by Emperor Hadrian, a Roman ruler known for his interest in Greek culture and his efforts to promote learning.

The library was part of Hadrian's broader initiative to blend Roman and Greek traditions, and it symbolized the cultural and intellectual exchange between the two civilizations.

Cultural Influence

The library was not just a place for storing books but a center of cultural and intellectual activity. It played a key role in the preservation and dissemination of knowledge, contributing to the rich tapestry of Greek and Roman cultural heritage.

The Odeon of Herodes Atticus: Athens' Iconic Amphitheater

Situated on the southern slopes of the Acropolis, the Odeon of Herodes Atticus stands as a testament to Athens' enduring cultural heritage. This ancient amphitheater, with its majestic stone facade and rich history, offers visitors an unparalleled glimpse into the artistic legacy of Greece.

Built in 161 AD by the affluent Roman senator Herodes Atticus, in memory of his beloved wife, Regilla, the Odeon remains one of the world's best-preserved ancient theaters and is still in use today, providing a unique bridge between the past and present.

A Journey Through Time

As you approach the Odeon, the first thing that strikes you is the imposing stone facade, which immediately transports you back to the grandeur of ancient Rome. The amphitheater was originally covered with a wooden roof made from cedar wood, an architectural marvel of its time.

Although the roof no longer exists, the theater itself is remarkably well-preserved. The semi-circular seating arrangement, constructed from Pentelic marble, remains mostly intact, giving you a vivid sense of the scale and grandeur that must have greeted audiences nearly two millennia ago.

The Optimal Time to Visit

Timing is everything when it comes to exploring the Odeon of Herodes Atticus. The best times to visit are either in the early morning or late afternoon. In the morning, the site is bathed in the soft light of the rising sun, offering a peaceful ambiance that's perfect for introspection and photography.

This is also when the crowds are at their smallest, allowing you to explore the amphitheater in relative solitude. Alternatively, visiting in the late afternoon allows you to experience the warm, golden hues of the sunset as they play off the ancient stone, creating a truly magical atmosphere.

Self-Guided vs. Guided Exploration

While you can certainly appreciate the Odeon on your own, a guided tour can enrich your experience significantly. Many expert guides in Athens offer tours that provide in-depth historical context, shedding light on the amphitheater's construction, its role in ancient Athenian society, and its evolution over the centuries.

A knowledgeable guide can bring the ancient ruins to life with stories of the Odeon's past, such as the performances it hosted, from classical Greek tragedies to Roman musical events.

The View from Above

One of the highlights of visiting the Odeon is the panoramic view from the upper tiers of the amphitheater. As you ascend the marble steps, you'll be rewarded with a breathtaking vista that stretches across Athens, with the Parthenon towering above and the sprawling city below.

This vantage point not only offers stunning photo opportunities but also provides a moment to reflect on the historical significance of the Acropolis complex, of which the Odeon is an integral part.

Attending a Performance

If your visit coincides with the annual Athens and Epidaurus Festival, usually held from June to August, you have the unique opportunity to experience the Odeon as it was meant to be: a living theater. The festival hosts a variety of performances, from classical music concerts to contemporary dance, all set against the backdrop of this ancient venue.

Attending a performance here is nothing short of magical, as the acoustics of the amphitheater are still exceptional, and the atmosphere is charged with the energy of countless performances that have taken place over the centuries.

Practical Information

The Odeon is easily accessible from the pedestrianized Dionysiou Areopagitou Street, which encircles the Acropolis. If you're already visiting the Acropolis Museum or the Parthenon, it's a short and pleasant walk to the amphitheater.

The site is open during the day for visitors, though specific hours can vary depending on the season and events. Tickets can be purchased on-site or online, and it's advisable to check the schedule in advance, especially if you plan to attend a performance.

Explore Byzantine and Christian Museum

Location: Vasilissis Sofias Avenue 22, Athens 106 75, Greece

Situated in the heart of Athens, the Byzantine and Christian Museum is a treasure trove of religious art and artifacts that offers a profound exploration of Greece's rich Christian heritage. Established in 1914, this museum houses one of the most important collections of Byzantine and post-Byzantine art in the world.

With over 30,000 exhibits spanning from the 3rd to the 20th century, the museum provides an unparalleled journey through the history of the Byzantine Empire and the evolution of Christianity in Greece.

A Historical Overview

The museum is housed in Villa Ilissia, a 19th-century mansion that once belonged to the Duchess of Placentia, Sophie de Marbois-Lebrun. The building itself is a work of art, blending classical and neo-Gothic architectural elements.

The museum's collection is displayed in a series of well-curated galleries that take visitors through different historical periods, offering insight into the religious, cultural, and social aspects of Byzantine and Christian life.

Highlights of the Collection

As you begin your tour, you'll be greeted by the museum's extensive collection of early Christian art, which includes stunning mosaics, frescoes, and icons.

These works of art not only reflect the religious devotion of the time but also the intricate craftsmanship that characterized Byzantine art. One of the standout pieces is a 5th-century mosaic depicting Christ, which showcases the transition from classical to Christian art.

The museum also boasts an impressive collection of icons, which are central to Orthodox Christian worship. These icons, some of which date back to the 12th century, are beautifully preserved and offer a glimpse into the spiritual life of the Byzantine Empire. Particularly noteworthy are the icons of the Virgin Mary and Christ Pantocrator, which are revered for their artistic and religious significance.

The museum's collection also includes a variety of everyday objects that provide insight into the daily lives of the Byzantine people. These include ceramics, textiles, and manuscripts, all of which reveal the sophistication of Byzantine society.

The museum also features a collection of religious vestments and ecclesiastical objects, such as chalices and crosses, which highlight the ritualistic aspects of Byzantine Christianity.

Thematic Exhibitions and Interactive Displays

One of the museum's strengths is its thematic exhibitions, which delve into specific aspects of Byzantine and Christian culture. These exhibitions often explore topics such as the role of women in Byzantine society, the significance of pilgrimage, and the impact of the Crusades on the Byzantine Empire.

The museum also utilizes interactive displays, including digital reconstructions and multimedia presentations, which bring the ancient world to life for visitors.

The Garden of the Museum

Before or after your visit to the museum, take some time to explore the beautiful garden that surrounds Villa Ilissia. The garden is designed to reflect the landscape of the Byzantine era, with plants and trees that were commonly found in monastic gardens.

It's a peaceful oasis in the bustling city, where you can relax and reflect on the rich history you've just explored.

Practical Information

The Byzantine and Christian Museum is conveniently located on Vasilissis Sofias Avenue, within walking distance of other major attractions such as the National Gallery and the Benaki Museum.

The museum is easily accessible by public transportation, with several bus and metro stops nearby. It's open daily, except for major holidays, and offers reduced admission for students, seniors, and groups.

Guided tours are available and highly recommended, as they provide deeper insight into the significance of the museum's collection. The museum also offers educational programs and workshops, making it a great destination for families and school groups.

Chapter Five
Cultural Experiences in Athens

Athens' Festivals: From Athens Epidaurus to Rockwave

Athens is a city where ancient history and vibrant modern culture intersect, and nowhere is this more evident than in its diverse array of festivals. From the classical grandeur of the Athens Epidaurus Festival to the contemporary beats of Rockwave, Athens offers a festival experience that caters to every taste.

These events not only showcase the city's rich cultural heritage but also its dynamic role as a modern metropolis. Here's the best way to explore some of Athens' most iconic festivals.

Athens Epidaurus Festival

Location: Various venues across Athens, including the Odeon of Herodes Atticus and Epidaurus Theater.

The Athens Epidaurus Festival is one of the oldest and most prestigious cultural events in Greece, celebrating its rich theatrical tradition and vibrant performing arts scene. Held annually from June to August, the festival features a diverse program of performances, including ancient Greek drama, contemporary theater, music concerts, and dance.

The festival's performances take place in some of Greece's most historic venues, including the Odeon of Herodes Atticus and the ancient theater of Epidaurus.

Best Way to Experience the Festival

To fully immerse yourself in the Athens Epidaurus Festival, start with a visit to the Odeon of Herodes Atticus, located at the foot of the Acropolis. This iconic amphitheater, with its stunning acoustics and majestic backdrop, offers an unforgettable setting for experiencing classical performances.

Whether it's a stirring rendition of a Greek tragedy or a contemporary dance performance, the atmosphere is electric.

For those willing to venture outside the city, a trip to the ancient theater of Epidaurus is a must. Located about two hours from Athens, this UNESCO World Heritage site is renowned for its unparalleled acoustics and stunning natural setting. Watching a performance here is a transcendent experience that transports you back to ancient Greece.

When planning your visit, it's advisable to book tickets in advance, as performances often sell out quickly, especially for well-known plays and musical events. Consider attending a mix of performances to experience both ancient and modern interpretations of Greek culture.

Rockwave Festival

Location: TerraVibe Park, Malakasa, approximately 40 km north of Athens.

For those with a taste for contemporary music, the Rockwave Festival is Athens' premier rock and alternative music event. Held annually in July, Rockwave attracts some of the biggest names in rock, indie, and electronic music from around the world.

The festival is set in TerraVibe Park, a large outdoor venue surrounded by nature, providing the perfect backdrop for a summer music festival.

Best Way to Experience the Festival

Getting to Rockwave is relatively easy, with regular shuttle buses running from central Athens to TerraVibe Park. If you prefer to drive, there is ample parking available, though it can get busy, so arriving early is recommended.

Once at the festival, immerse yourself in the energetic atmosphere as you move between the different stages. Rockwave typically features multiple stages, each hosting a variety of acts, from internationally acclaimed headliners to up-and-coming artists.

The diversity of the lineup ensures that there's something for everyone, whether you're a die-hard rock fan or simply looking to enjoy the festival vibe.

To make the most of your Rockwave experience, consider camping at TerraVibe Park. The festival offers on-site camping, which allows you to fully embrace the festival spirit and enjoy late-night performances and after-parties.

Alternatively, there are plenty of hotels and guesthouses in the nearby towns of Malakasa and Afidnes if you prefer a more comfortable stay.

Attending Both Festivals

For the ultimate cultural experience in Athens, plan your visit to coincide with both the Athens Epidaurus Festival and Rockwave. This will allow you to experience the full spectrum of Athenian culture, from its ancient theatrical traditions to its modern music scene.

Both festivals reflect different aspects of Athens' cultural identity, and attending both offers a unique opportunity to see how the city honors its past while embracing the present.

When attending both festivals, it's important to plan your itinerary carefully. The Athens Epidaurus Festival's performances are often scheduled in the evenings, while Rockwave runs throughout the day and night, so it's possible to attend events at both.

Be sure to leave some time in between to explore the city's other cultural offerings, such as its museums, galleries, and historical sites.

Practical Information

Both festivals are highly popular, so it's essential to book tickets and accommodation well in advance. Tickets for the Athens Epidaurus Festival can be purchased online through the festival's official website, while Rockwave tickets are available through various online ticketing platforms.

For the Athens Epidaurus Festival, consider renting a car if you plan to visit the theater of Epidaurus, as it's located outside the city and public transport options are limited. For Rockwave, the shuttle service from Athens is convenient and saves you the hassle of driving.

Visiting Local Workshops

Athens, a city renowned for its ancient history and vibrant culture, offers visitors the opportunity to delve into its rich artisanal traditions. Beyond the iconic landmarks and bustling streets, the heart of Athenian culture can be found in its local workshops, where craftsmen and women continue to practice the age-old skills of pottery, jewelry making, and other traditional craft.

Visiting these workshops provides a unique, hands-on experience that connects you with the soul of Athens and offers a deeper understanding of its cultural heritage.

Discovering Pottery Workshops

Pottery is one of Greece's oldest and most revered crafts, with roots that stretch back to ancient times. The pottery workshops of Athens continue this tradition, producing both functional and decorative pieces that are sought after by collectors and visitors alike.

Best Areas to Explore: One of the best areas to explore pottery workshops is in the neighborhood of Psiri, known for its vibrant arts scene. Here, you'll find small, family-run workshops where artisans still use traditional methods to create beautiful ceramics.

Many of these workshops offer demonstrations, allowing you to see the entire process, from molding the clay to painting the intricate designs that are characteristic of Greek pottery.

Interactive Experience: Many workshops offer pottery classes where you can try your hand at creating your own piece of art. These classes are a fantastic way to engage with the craft, guided by expert potters who share their knowledge and passion.

It's a hands-on experience that not only teaches you the techniques but also allows you to bring home a unique, handmade souvenir.

Exploring Jewelry Workshops

Greek jewelry is renowned for its intricate designs and the use of precious metals and stones. The tradition of jewelry making in Athens dates back to ancient times, and today, you can still find master jewelers who craft exquisite pieces using techniques passed down through generations.

Where to Go: The area around Monastiraki and Plaka is home to some of Athens' best jewelry workshops. These neighborhoods, with their narrow streets and historic ambiance, are perfect for discovering small studios where artisans create everything from modern interpretations of ancient designs to contemporary pieces that reflect current trends.

Personalized Experience: Visiting a jewelry workshop gives you the chance to see the meticulous process of crafting jewelry up close. Some workshops even offer the option to commission custom pieces, where you can work directly with the jeweler to design something that is uniquely yours.

This personalized experience is not only memorable but also results in a piece of jewelry that carries a story and a connection to Athens.

Traditional Crafts: Weaving, Embroidery, and More

Beyond pottery and jewelry, Athens is also a hub for other traditional crafts such as weaving, embroidery, and leatherwork. These crafts are integral to Greek culture, with each piece telling a story of the country's history, folklore, and regional diversity.

Workshops to Visit: In the district of Anafiotika, located under the shadow of the Acropolis, you can find workshops specializing in traditional Greek textiles. Here, artisans produce handwoven fabrics and intricate embroidery that are true works of art. These workshops often sell their creations directly to visitors, making it a great place to purchase authentic, handmade textiles.

Another craft worth exploring is leatherwork. The area around Ermou Street is known for its leather workshops, where skilled craftsmen create everything from sandals to handbags, using techniques that have been perfected over centuries.

These leather goods are not only stylish but also durable, making them a practical and beautiful souvenir.

Engaging with Artisans: What makes visiting these workshops particularly special is the opportunity to engage with the artisans themselves. Many of these craftsmen and women are happy to share the stories behind their work, explaining the significance of the designs, the materials they use, and the traditions they uphold.

This interaction adds a personal dimension to your experience, giving you a deeper appreciation for the craft and the cultural heritage it represents.

Practical Tips for Visiting Workshops

When planning your visits to local workshops, it's a good idea to research ahead of time. Some workshops operate on specific hours, and it's often best to visit in the morning when the artisans are most likely to be working.

Also,while many workshops are open to walk-ins, arranging a visit or class in advance can ensure you get a more personalized experience.

It's also worth considering bringing cash, as some of the smaller, traditional workshops may not accept credit cards. And don't forget to leave room in your luggage for the treasures you'll undoubtedly want to bring home!

Traditional Greek Music and Dance Performances

Athens, with its deep historical roots and rich cultural tapestry, is a city where the echoes of ancient traditions blend seamlessly with vibrant modern life. Among the most captivating aspects of Greek culture are its traditional music and dance performances.

These cultural expressions are not just entertainment; they are a window into the soul of Greece, telling stories of love, struggle, joy, and community that have been passed down through generations.

Rebetiko: The Sound of the Streets

Rebetiko music, often described as the Greek blues, originated in the early 20th century among the urban poor. Its lyrics often speak of the hardships and passions of life, set to melodies played on the bouzouki, guitar, and baglama. Rebetiko is deeply emotional and has a raw, authentic feel that resonates with listeners on a profound level.

Where to Experience Rebetiko: For an authentic rebetiko experience, head to the neighborhoods of Psiri or Exarcheia, where you'll find cozy music venues known as rebetadika. These intimate spaces are perfect for listening to live rebetiko performances, where musicians play just a few feet away from the audience, creating a powerful and immersive atmosphere.

Venues like **Stoa Athanaton** or **Rebetiki Istoria** are iconic spots where you can listen to some of the best rebetiko in Athens.

In these settings, the music is often accompanied by food and drink, with plates of meze (small dishes) and glasses of ouzo enhancing the experience. The performances usually start late and go on until the early hours of the morning, making for a truly unforgettable night.

Greek Folk Dance: A Celebration of Tradition

Greek folk dances are as varied as the country's regions, each with its own style and rhythm. These dances are often performed in a circle, symbolizing unity and community, and are an integral part of celebrations such as weddings, festivals, and religious holidays.

Best Venues for Folk Dance: The **Dora Stratou Dance Theatre**, located on Philopappou Hill, is the premier venue for traditional Greek dance in Athens. Established in 1953, this open-air theater offers nightly performances from May to September, showcasing a wide variety of dances from all over Greece. The dancers, dressed in traditional costumes, perform with live music, creating a vibrant and colorful spectacle against the backdrop of the Acropolis.

If you prefer a more interactive experience, consider visiting one of the many tavernas in Plaka, the historic district of Athens. These tavernas often feature live music with opportunities for guests to join in the dancing.

Participating in a syrtaki or kalamatianos dance, even as a beginner, is a joyous way to connect with Greek culture.

The Bouzoukia: A Night of Glamour and Music

For a more contemporary take on traditional music, spend a night at one of Athens' famous bouzoukia clubs. These large venues are dedicated to laïko, a genre of Greek popular music that has its roots in traditional folk music but incorporates modern elements.

The bouzoukia are known for their extravagant performances, where famous Greek singers perform to packed houses.

Popular Bouzoukia in Athens: Venues like **Posidonio** and **Fever** are among the most famous bouzoukia clubs in Athens. A night at the bouzoukia is a lively, glamorous affair, with patrons often participating by singing along, dancing, and throwing flowers at the stage—a unique custom that adds to the festive atmosphere.

While the music is more modern than rebetiko or folk, the bouzoukia experience is a deep dive into contemporary Greek culture. It's an event where you can see how traditional Greek music has evolved and adapted to modern tastes while still retaining its core emotional impact.

Tips for Enjoying Traditional Performances

When planning to attend traditional music or dance performances in Athens, it's wise to book your tickets or make reservations in advance, especially for popular venues like the Dora Stratou Theatre or bouzoukia clubs, which can get fully booked quickly.

Dress codes vary depending on the venue. Rebetadika and tavernas are generally casual, while bouzoukia clubs may require more formal attire. In any setting, a comfortable outfit that allows for dancing is a good choice.

If you're interested in participating in the dances, don't be afraid to join in. Greek dances are communal and welcoming, and locals are often happy to show you the steps. Remember, the spirit of the dance lies in the joy and togetherness it fosters, not in perfect execution.

Chapter Six
Food and Drink

Traditional Greek Cuisine: Must-Try Dishes and Local Flavors

Greek cuisine is an exquisite tapestry woven from centuries of history, culture, and geography. In Athens, this culinary heritage is vividly brought to life through a diverse array of dishes that reflect the nation's love for fresh ingredients, bold flavors, and communal dining.

Moussaka

Often hailed as Greece's national dish, Moussaka is a hearty, oven-baked casserole that layers eggplant, minced meat (typically beef or lamb), and a creamy béchamel sauce. The eggplant slices are usually fried or grilled to tender perfection, while the meat is seasoned with a blend of aromatic spices such as cinnamon and nutmeg, giving the dish a warm, comforting flavor.

The béchamel, made from butter, flour, and milk, is enriched with eggs and cheese, creating a velvety topping that contrasts beautifully with the savory meat and vegetable layers beneath. Moussaka is often enjoyed with a side of Greek salad or a dollop of tangy yogurt.

Souvlaki

Souvlaki is the quintessential Greek street food. It consists of skewered and grilled pieces of meat, typically pork, chicken, or lamb, served with pita bread and a variety of accompaniments. The meat is marinated in olive oil, lemon juice, and a blend of herbs like oregano, garlic, and rosemary before being grilled to perfection.

Souvlaki is usually accompanied by tzatziki, a refreshing yogurt-based sauce with cucumber and garlic, and garnished with fresh vegetables such as tomatoes, onions, and lettuce. It's a perfect dish for a quick, flavorful bite while exploring the vibrant streets of Athens.

Gyro

Similar to souvlaki, Gyro is another popular Greek fast food. It features meat that is cooked on a vertical rotisserie, typically pork or chicken, and served in a pita bread with an array of toppings. The meat is seasoned with a mix of spices and herbs, then thinly sliced and topped with tzatziki, tomatoes, onions, and sometimes fries.

Gyro is a savory, satisfying meal that captures the essence of Greek street food and is a must-try for anyone visiting Athens.

Spanakopita

Spanakopita, or spinach pie, is a classic Greek pastry that combines spinach, feta cheese, onions, and dill, all encased in layers of crispy, buttery phyllo dough. The filling is rich and flavorful, with the feta cheese providing a tangy contrast to the earthy spinach.

This savory pie is often enjoyed as a snack or appetizer and is a staple in many Greek households. The flaky texture of the phyllo and the combination of ingredients make Spanakopita a delightful treat that showcases Greece's love for both simplicity and flavor.

Dolmades

Dolmades are grape leaves stuffed with a mixture of rice, pine nuts, and herbs, often served with a lemony sauce. These little parcels are cooked until tender and can be enjoyed warm or at room temperature. The filling is typically seasoned with dill, mint, and sometimes ground meat, offering a refreshing and aromatic flavor profile.

Dolmades are a traditional dish that embodies the Greek emphasis on fresh, wholesome ingredients and are commonly served as part of a meze platter.

Tzatziki

Tzatziki is a quintessential Greek dip made from strained yogurt, cucumber, garlic, olive oil, and dill. It is incredibly refreshing and pairs perfectly with grilled meats, pita bread, or as a cooling side to spicier dishes.

The yogurt base provides a creamy texture, while the cucumber adds a crisp crunch, and the garlic and dill contribute a fragrant, tangy flavor. Tzatziki is often enjoyed as an appetizer or a condiment, making it a versatile staple in Greek cuisine.

Greek Salad

Greek salad, or Horiatiki, is a vibrant, refreshing dish that epitomizes the Greek love for fresh, seasonal produce. It features juicy tomatoes, crisp cucumbers, red onions, Kalamata olives, and slabs of creamy feta cheese, all drizzled with extra virgin olive oil and seasoned with oregano.

The combination of flavors and textures makes Greek salad a perfect accompaniment to any meal, providing a burst of freshness and a taste of the Mediterranean.

Baklava

For a sweet ending, Baklava is an indulgent Greek dessert made from layers of phyllo dough filled with chopped nuts and sweetened with honey or syrup. The layers of dough are baked until golden and crispy, while the nut filling provides a rich, satisfying crunch.

The sweet syrup infuses the baklava with a deliciously sticky sweetness that complements the nutty filling. Baklava is a popular treat throughout Greece and is a delightful way to experience Greek pastry traditions.

Best Restaurants and Taverns in Athens

Athens boasts a rich culinary landscape that spans from beloved street food stalls to prestigious fine dining establishments.

In case you're in the mood for a quick and flavorful bite or a sophisticated gastronomic adventure, Athens has something to offer every palate.

Kostas

For an authentic taste of Greek street food, Kostas is a must-visit. Known for its superb souvlaki, this spot is a local favorite.

The souvlaki, skewers of marinated and grilled meat served in warm pita bread with fresh vegetables and tzatziki, is a quintessential Greek street food experience. The simplicity and quality of the food make it a standout choice for a quick, satisfying meal.

Address: 5 Pentelis Street, Athens 10557 **Opening Hours:** Monday to Saturday, 11:00 AM – 11:00 PM; Closed on Sundays

Highlights: Kostas is celebrated for its expertly grilled souvlaki and fast service, perfect for a flavorful meal on the go.

Ta Karamanlidika Tou Fani

Ta Karamanlidika Tou Fani offers a taste of traditional Greek charcuterie and meze. The menu features a variety of cured meats, cheeses, and traditional dishes, all served in a charming, rustic setting.

The eatery's focus on high-quality ingredients and authentic flavors provides a delightful dive into Greek culinary traditions.

Address: 1 Sokratous Street, Athens 10552
Opening Hours: Monday to Saturday, 9:00 AM – 11:00 PM; Closed on Sundays

Highlights: Renowned for its cured meats and artisanal cheeses, Ta Karamanlidika Tou Fani is ideal for enjoying a selection of traditional Greek meze.

Spondi

Spondi is a beacon of fine dining in Athens, renowned for its two Michelin stars and exceptional cuisine. The restaurant offers an exquisite tasting menu that combines Greek and Mediterranean flavors with modern culinary techniques.

Each dish is meticulously prepared using the finest seasonal ingredients, providing a sophisticated dining experience.

Address: 5 Pirée Street, Athens 11635
Opening Hours: Tuesday to Saturday, 7:00 PM – 11:00 PM; Closed on Sundays and Mondays

Highlights: Spondi's elegant atmosphere and creative tasting menus make it a top choice for a luxurious dining experience.

Funky Gourmet

Funky Gourmet is known for its avant-garde approach to Greek cuisine. With a Michelin star, the restaurant offers inventive tasting menus that push the boundaries of traditional Greek cooking.

The dishes are crafted with an emphasis on creativity and presentation, providing a unique and memorable dining experience.

Address: 13-15 Parthenonos Street, Athens 11854
Opening Hours: Tuesday to Saturday, 7:00 PM – 11:00 PM; Closed on Sundays and Mondays

Highlights: Funky Gourmet's imaginative dishes and modern setting make it a perfect spot for exploring innovative Greek cuisine.

Oineas Restaurant

Oineas Restaurant offers a warm and rustic dining experience with a menu full of classic Greek dishes. The restaurant serves generous portions of grilled meats, seafood, and traditional meze, all prepared with a focus on authentic flavors.

The inviting atmosphere makes it a great place to enjoy a hearty Greek meal.

Address: 24 Karaiskaki Street, Athens 10554
Opening Hours: Monday to Saturday, 12:00 PM – 12:00 AM; Closed on Sundays

Highlights: Oineas is known for its flavorful grilled octopus and lamb chops, providing a traditional Greek dining experience in a cozy setting.

Strofi

Strofi offers a fantastic combination of delicious Greek cuisine and breathtaking views of the Acropolis. The menu features a variety of traditional Greek dishes, including grilled meats, fresh fish, and savory appetizers.

The outdoor terrace provides an ideal setting to enjoy a meal while taking in the iconic views of Athens.

Address: 25 G. Makri Street, Athens 11742
Opening Hours: Monday to Sunday, 12:00 PM – 11:00 PM

Highlights: Strofi's stunning views and excellent food make it a popular choice for both locals and visitors looking to enjoy Greek cuisine with a scenic backdrop.

Diporto

Diporto is a hidden gem that offers an authentic taste of Greek home cooking. Located in a subterranean space, the tavern serves traditional dishes like moussaka and pastitsio, prepared with a focus on quality and tradition.

The restaurant's unpretentious charm adds to its appeal, providing a genuine Greek dining experience.

Address: 8 Sokratous Street, Athens 10552
Opening Hours: Monday to Saturday, 1:00 PM – 11:00 PM; Closed on Sundays

Highlights: Diporto's cozy atmosphere and traditional dishes make it a unique spot for experiencing authentic Greek cuisine.

Aleria

Aleria is a stylish restaurant that offers a contemporary take on Greek cuisine. The menu features modern interpretations of traditional dishes, crafted with high-quality ingredients and innovative techniques.

The restaurant's chic decor and refined dishes provide a sophisticated dining experience.

Address: 57 Platia Eleftherias Street, Athens 11474
Opening Hours: Tuesday to Saturday, 1:00 PM – 3:00 PM, 8:00 PM – 11:00 PM; Closed on Sundays and Mondays

Highlights: Aleria's elegant setting and creative dishes make it a top choice for a refined dining experience in Athens.

Exploring Varvakios Agora and Beyond

Athens, a city steeped in history and culture, offers a vibrant food market scene that reflects its rich culinary heritage. Exploring these markets provides an immersive experience into local life, showcasing everything from fresh produce to traditional delicacies.

Among the most notable is Varvakios Agora, but there are also other markets worth exploring for a comprehensive taste of Athens.

Varvakios Agora (Central Market)

Address: 42 Athinas Street, Athens 10551
Opening Hours: Monday to Saturday, 7:00 AM – 3:00 PM; Closed on Sundays

Varvakios Agora, also known as the Central Market, is the heart of Athens' food scene. This bustling marketplace, located in the city center, is a feast for the senses.

It offers a wide array of fresh produce, meats, fish, and local delicacies. The market is divided into sections, each dedicated to different types of goods:

Meat Section: Here, you'll find a diverse selection of meats, from traditional cuts to exotic offerings. The vendors are known for their expertise and are happy to share recommendations or tips on cooking.

Fish Section: Fresh seafood is a highlight of Varvakios Agora. The fishmongers offer everything from locally caught fish to imported shellfish, ensuring a wide variety of options for seafood enthusiasts.

Produce Section: Vibrant stalls display a colorful assortment of fruits and vegetables, including seasonal and exotic varieties. This section is ideal for picking up fresh ingredients and experiencing the local flavors.

Spice and Olive Oil Stalls: The market also features stalls selling aromatic spices, herbs, and high-quality olive oils. These ingredients are essential to Greek cuisine and offer a taste of authentic Greek flavors.

Exploring Varvakios Agora is more than just a shopping trip; it's an opportunity to engage with local vendors, sample fresh products, and experience the vibrant atmosphere of one of Athens' most iconic markets.

Modiano and Kapani Markets

Address: Modiano Market: 52-54 Ermou Street, Thessaloniki **Kapani Market:** Located near Modiano Market, Thessaloniki **Opening Hours:** Vary by stall; generally open daily from early morning until late afternoon

Although located in Thessaloniki rather than Athens, Modiano and Kapani Markets are worth mentioning for their relevance to Greek food culture. These markets are renowned for their diverse offerings, including fresh produce, meats, fish, and local specialties.

If you're traveling beyond Athens, these markets provide a similar vibrant experience as Varvakios Agora, showcasing the regional culinary traditions of Northern Greece.

Laiki Agora (Neighborhood Markets)

Throughout Athens, Laiki Agora refers to neighborhood markets that pop up weekly in various districts.

These markets offer a more localized experience compared to the Central Market, with vendors selling fresh produce, homemade goods, and artisanal products. Some notable Laiki Agoras include:

Kifisia Laiki Agora: Located in the Kifisia district, this market features a range of fresh produce, local cheeses, and baked goods.

Kolonaki Laiki Agora: Situated in the upscale Kolonaki neighborhood, this market offers high-quality ingredients and gourmet products.

Opening Hours: Generally, these markets operate on specific days of the week, typically from early morning to early afternoon. It's best to check the schedule for the specific neighborhood market you plan to visit.

Athens Farmers' Market

Address: Varies by location
Opening Hours: Typically open on weekends, with hours varying by market

Athens Farmers' Markets, held in various locations throughout the city, focus on organic and locally-produced goods. These markets offer a range of fresh fruits, vegetables, dairy products, and artisanal items.

They are an excellent place to find high-quality, organic products and to support local farmers and producers.

Psiri and Monastiraki Flea Markets

Address: Psiri: Located near Monastiraki Square
Opening Hours: Monday to Saturday, 10:00 AM – 6:00 PM

The Psiri and Monastiraki areas are known for their vibrant flea markets, where you can find a mix of food stalls, antiques, and crafts.

These markets offer a more eclectic shopping experience, with food vendors selling everything from traditional Greek snacks to international street food.

Greek Wines and Spirits: The Athens Wine Tasting Scene

Athens, a city with a rich cultural and culinary heritage, offers a vibrant wine and spirits scene that reflects Greece's storied vinous traditions. From ancient vineyards to modern wine bars, Athens provides numerous opportunities to explore Greek wines and spirits.

Kava Pyrgou

Address: 14 Kifisias Avenue, Athens 115 26
Opening Hours: Monday to Friday, 9:00 AM – 8:00 PM; Saturday, 9:00 AM – 4:00 PM; Closed on Sundays

Kava Pyrgou is a well-regarded wine shop and tasting venue offering an extensive selection of Greek wines. The store is known for its curated collection of wines from across Greece's diverse wine regions, including Santorini, Naoussa, and Nemea.

Here, you can explore a range of local and international labels, with knowledgeable staff available to guide you through the tasting process.

Highlights: Kava Pyrgou hosts regular wine tastings and events, allowing visitors to sample various wines and learn about the unique characteristics of Greek viticulture. The store's selection includes both well-known and boutique labels, providing a comprehensive overview of Greek wines.

Oinoscent

Address: 6 Kallidromiou Street, Athens 106 80
Opening Hours: Monday to Saturday, 12:00 PM – 11:00 PM; Closed on Sundays

Oinoscent is a trendy wine bar and restaurant that focuses on Greek wines and artisanal cheeses. With an extensive wine list featuring selections from Greece's top wineries, Oinoscent offers a refined setting for tasting and pairing.

The bar's knowledgeable staff can provide recommendations and insights into the wine regions and varieties featured.

Highlights: Oinoscent's menu includes a variety of Greek wines by the glass, allowing you to sample different styles and regions. The wine list is complemented by a selection of gourmet cheeses and charcuterie, making it an excellent spot for a relaxed and informative wine tasting experience.

Dionysos Zonar's

Address: 5-7 Dionysiou Areopagitou Street, Athens 11742
Opening Hours: Monday to Sunday, 12:00 PM – 12:00 AM

Located near the Acropolis, Dionysos Zonar's combines stunning views with a comprehensive wine list. This upscale restaurant and wine bar offers a wide range of Greek and international wines, carefully selected to pair with a menu of fine dining options.

The elegant setting and knowledgeable staff enhance the wine tasting experience.

Highlights: Dionysos Zonar's features a curated wine list with a focus on Greek wines, including some rare and high-quality labels. The restaurant's prime location and sophisticated ambiance make it a great place to enjoy wine with a view of the Acropolis.

Kifisia Wine Bar

Address: 1 Kifisias Avenue, Kifisia, Athens 145 62
Opening Hours: Monday to Saturday, 12:00 PM – 12:00 AM; Closed on Sundays

Kifisia Wine Bar is a popular spot for wine enthusiasts in the upscale Kifisia neighborhood. The bar offers an extensive selection of Greek wines, including both well-known and boutique labels.

The cozy atmosphere and knowledgeable staff make it an ideal place for discovering new wines and enjoying a relaxed tasting session.

Highlights: Kifisia Wine Bar features a diverse wine list with options for both classic and emerging Greek varieties. The bar also offers wine pairing recommendations and hosts events that highlight different wine regions and styles.

Greek Wine Museum

Address: 9 Kolokotroni Street, Athens 105 62
Opening Hours: Monday to Friday, 10:00 AM – 6:00 PM; Saturday, 10:00 AM – 3:00 PM; Closed on Sundays

The Greek Wine Museum provides a deeper understanding of Greece's winemaking history and traditions. While not a tasting venue itself, the museum offers educational exhibits about Greek wine regions, historical winemaking practices, and the evolution of Greek viticulture.

It's an excellent starting point for those interested in learning more about the background of Greek wines.

Highlights: The museum's exhibits include historical artifacts, interactive displays, and informative panels about Greece's winemaking heritage. It provides valuable context for appreciating the wines you encounter in Athens.

Athens Wine Tasting Experiences

Several companies in Athens offer curated wine tasting experiences, often including guided tours of local wineries, tastings of regional wines, and food pairings.

These experiences can be tailored to various interests, whether you're new to Greek wines or a seasoned enthusiast.

Highlights: Wine tasting tours provide hands-on experiences with Greek wines, often including visits to vineyards and interactions with winemakers. These tours offer a comprehensive look at Greek wine culture and production methods.

Greek Spirits

Greek spirits such as ouzo and tsipouro are integral to the country's drinking culture. Ouzo, an anise-flavored aperitif, is often enjoyed with meze, while tsipouro, a pomace brandy, is typically served with a variety of appetizers.

Many bars and restaurants in Athens offer these traditional spirits, providing a taste of Greek drinking customs.

Chapter Seven
Shopping in Athens

Visit Plaka and Monastiraki Flea Markets

Athens, with its rich history and vibrant culture, offers a shopping experience that ranges from elegant boutiques to bustling markets. Among the most charming and eclectic shopping destinations are the Plaka and Monastiraki Flea Markets.

These areas are perfect for discovering unique souvenirs and artisanal goods, reflecting the city's blend of ancient tradition and contemporary style.

Plaka District: A Historic Shopping Experience

Location: Plaka, Athens 10558
Opening Hours: Shops generally open daily from 10:00 AM to 8:00 PM, with varying hours for individual stores.

Plaka, often referred to as Athens' "old town," is a picturesque neighborhood nestled at the foot of the Acropolis. It's renowned for its narrow, winding streets, neoclassical architecture, and vibrant shopping scene.

Walking through Plaka is like stepping back in time, with its blend of traditional Greek charm and modern retail.

Shopping Highlights:

Traditional Souvenirs: Plaka is an ideal place to pick up classic Greek souvenirs such as handmade ceramics, intricately designed jewelry, and traditional Greek textiles. Shops like *The Greek Shop* offer a range of products from embroidered tablecloths to hand-painted plates.

Artisanal Goods: The area is dotted with small boutiques selling artisanal goods. *Martha's Artisan Souvenirs* is known for its handcrafted leather products and locally produced olive oil, while *Plaka Gallery* offers a selection of unique art pieces and crafts from local artists.

Handmade Jewelry: For those interested in jewelry, *Plaka Jewelry* showcases an array of handmade pieces that blend traditional Greek designs with contemporary styles. Each item is crafted with attention to detail, making it a memorable keepsake.

Local Markets: The *Plaka Market*, situated in the heart of the district, provides a lively atmosphere where you can find local products such as spices, herbs, and traditional Greek sweets.

Plaka's charming streets are perfect for leisurely strolling and discovering hidden gems. The area's combination of historical ambiance and modern shopping makes it a unique destination for visitors seeking authentic Greek experiences.

Monastiraki Flea Market: A Treasure Trove of Finds

Location: Monastiraki, Athens 10555
Opening Hours: Monday to Saturday, 10:00 AM – 8:00 PM; Closed on Sundays

The Monastiraki Flea Market, located in the vibrant Monastiraki neighborhood, is one of Athens' most famous and bustling markets. Known for its eclectic mix of goods and lively atmosphere, it's a must-visit for those looking to explore Athens' diverse shopping scene.

Shopping Highlights:

Vintage Finds: The Monastiraki Flea Market is renowned for its vintage and second-hand goods. You can find everything from antique furniture and vintage clothing to retro collectibles.

Antique Agora specializes in antique furniture and artifacts, while *Vintage Alley* is a treasure trove for retro clothing and accessories.

Local Artisans: The market features a variety of stalls selling handcrafted items. Look out for local artisans showcasing their work, including handwoven textiles, pottery, and traditional Greek crafts. *Artisan's Corner* offers a range of handcrafted jewelry and home décor items.

Souvenirs and Gifts: For unique souvenirs, the market has numerous stalls selling Greek-themed products such as olive oil, honey, and locally produced wines. *Greek Treasures* is a popular stall for its wide selection of traditional Greek souvenirs and artisanal goods.

Food and Snacks: The market is also a great place to sample local Greek street food. Stalls offer delicious options like souvlaki, fresh olives, and Greek pastries.

Souvlaki King and *Baklava Bazaar* are local favorites where you can enjoy authentic Greek snacks while shopping.

Bargain Hunting: The Flea Market is known for its vibrant atmosphere and the opportunity to haggle for deals. Vendors are often open to negotiation, making it a fun place to find bargains and unique items.

Monastiraki Flea Market provides a dynamic shopping experience with its mix of new and old, high-end and affordable. The market's lively ambiance, combined with its wide array of goods, ensures that there's something for everyone.

Tips for Visiting

Cash: While many vendors accept cards, having cash on hand can be useful for smaller purchases and haggling in the Flea Market.

Comfortable Shoes: Both Plaka and Monastiraki involve a lot of walking, so comfortable footwear is essential.

Bargaining: In the Monastiraki Flea Market, don't be afraid to negotiate prices, especially for antiques and vintage items.

Explore the Luxury Boutiques in Kolonaki

Kolonaki, an upscale district in Athens, is renowned for its elegant boutiques and luxury shopping experience. Nestled in the heart of the city, this neighborhood offers a sophisticated retail environment where high-end fashion, exclusive accessories, and premium goods are the norm.

Lalunà Boutique

Address: 22 Skoufa Street, Kolonaki, Athens 10673
Opening Hours: Monday to Friday, 10:00 AM – 8:00 PM; Saturday, 10:00 AM – 6:00 PM; Closed on Sundays

Lalunà Boutique is a prestigious fashion destination known for its curated selection of high-end clothing and accessories. The boutique features collections from renowned Greek and international designers, offering a blend of classic elegance and contemporary style.

From luxurious evening gowns to stylish casual wear, Lalunà provides a sophisticated shopping experience.

Highlights: The boutique's exclusive collections and personalized service make it a top choice for those seeking premium fashion items. The store's chic interior and attentive staff enhance the luxury shopping experience.

Kastner & Öhler

Address: 7 Kolonaki Square, Athens 10673
Opening Hours: Monday to Friday, 10:00 AM – 8:00 PM; Saturday, 10:00 AM – 6:00 PM; Closed on Sundays

Kastner & Öhler is an iconic name in luxury retail, offering a wide range of designer fashion, accessories, and lifestyle products.

This upscale department store features an array of high-end brands, including both global fashion houses and exclusive labels. The store's elegant ambiance and extensive selection make it a premier destination for luxury shopping.

Highlights: Kastner & Öhler's reputation for quality and service ensures a refined shopping experience. The store's diverse product range caters to various tastes and styles, providing something for every luxury shopper.

Dior

Address: 1 Kolonaki Square, Athens 10673
Opening Hours: Monday to Friday, 10:00 AM – 8:00 PM; Saturday, 10:00 AM – 6:00 PM; Closed on Sundays

The Dior boutique in Kolonaki is a must-visit for lovers of haute couture and luxury fashion. Known for its timeless elegance and iconic designs, Dior offers a range of high-end clothing, accessories, and fragrances.

The boutique's refined interior reflects the brand's commitment to luxury and sophistication.

Highlights: Dior's Kolonaki location provides a glamorous shopping experience with personalized service and exclusive collections. The boutique is perfect for finding elegant fashion pieces and classic accessories.

Chanel

Address: 15 Kolonaki Square, Athens 10673
Opening Hours: Monday to Friday, 10:00 AM – 8:00 PM; Saturday, 10:00 AM – 6:00 PM; Closed on Sundays

Chanel's boutique in Kolonaki offers an unparalleled selection of luxury fashion and accessories. Renowned for its iconic designs and timeless elegance, Chanel provides a range of high-end clothing, handbags, and jewelry.

The boutique's sophisticated atmosphere and exclusive offerings make it a premier destination for luxury shoppers.

Highlights: Chanel's Kolonaki store is known for its exquisite product range and exceptional service. It's an ideal place for those seeking classic, high-quality fashion items and accessories.

Louis Vuitton

Address: 10 Kolonaki Square, Athens 10673
Opening Hours: Monday to Friday, 10:00 AM – 8:00 PM; Saturday, 10:00 AM – 6:00 PM; Closed on Sundays

The Louis Vuitton boutique in Kolonaki represents the pinnacle of luxury and craftsmanship. Known for its iconic monogram bags and high-end fashion, Louis Vuitton offers a range of exclusive products, including leather goods, clothing, and accessories. The boutique's elegant design and premium selection provide a top-tier shopping experience.

Highlights: Louis Vuitton's Kolonaki location offers personalized service and a wide range of luxury items, making it a top choice for those seeking high-quality fashion and accessories.

Bvlgari

Address: 6 Kolonaki Square, Athens 10673
Opening Hours: Monday to Friday, 10:00 AM – 8:00 PM; Saturday, 10:00 AM – 6:00 PM; Closed on Sundays

Bvlgari's boutique in Kolonaki is renowned for its exquisite jewelry and luxury watches. The store features a collection of elegant designs, from timeless pieces to contemporary creations.

The boutique's sophisticated ambiance and exceptional craftsmanship make it a premier destination for high-end jewelry and accessories.

Highlights: Bvlgari's Kolonaki location is known for its stunning jewelry collections and impeccable service, providing a luxurious shopping experience for those seeking fine craftsmanship and elegance.

Hermès

Address: 8 Kolonaki Square, Athens 10673
Opening Hours: Monday to Friday, 10:00 AM – 8:00 PM; Saturday, 10:00 AM – 6:00 PM; Closed on Sundays

Hermès offers a luxurious shopping experience with its renowned selection of high-end fashion and accessories. Known for its iconic scarves, leather goods, and timeless designs, Hermès provides a range of premium products in a refined setting.

The boutique's attention to detail and exceptional service make it a top choice for luxury shoppers.

Highlights: Hermès' Kolonaki boutique is celebrated for its elegant products and personalized service, offering a sophisticated shopping experience for those seeking classic luxury items.

Tips for Shopping in Kolonaki

Appointments: For personalized service and to ensure availability of specific items, consider making appointments at high-end boutiques, especially for special collections.

Fashion Events: Keep an eye out for special fashion events or trunk shows, which often take place in Kolonaki's luxury stores.

Etiquette: Luxury shopping in Kolonaki often involves a more formal shopping experience. Dress smartly and be prepared for a higher level of customer service.

Best Places to Buy Greek Jewelry and Art

Athens is a treasure trove for those seeking exquisite Greek jewelry and art. The city boasts a rich tradition of craftsmanship and artistic expression, reflected in its range of galleries and boutique stores.

Greece & Beyond

Address: 16 Mavromihali Street, Kolonaki, Athens 10679
Opening Hours: Monday to Friday, 10:00 AM – 8:00 PM; Saturday, 10:00 AM – 6:00 PM; Closed on Sundays

Greece & Beyond is a high-end boutique specializing in Greek jewelry and artisanal crafts. The store features a curated selection of unique jewelry pieces inspired by ancient Greek designs and modern trends.

You'll find handcrafted items made from precious metals and gemstones, each reflecting Greek heritage and artistry.

Highlights: The boutique offers pieces from well-known Greek designers, providing a range of styles from classic to contemporary. It's an ideal place to find elegant jewelry that combines traditional craftsmanship with modern aesthetics.

Folk Art Museum Shop

Address: 22 Kydathinaion Street, Plaka, Athens 10558
Opening Hours: Monday to Saturday, 9:00 AM – 7:00 PM; Closed on Sundays

Located next to the Museum of Greek Folk Art, this shop is a great place to find traditional Greek crafts and artworks. The shop features a range of items, including handmade jewelry, pottery, and textiles, showcasing the rich folk art traditions of Greece.

Highlights: The Folk Art Museum Shop offers a variety of authentic Greek crafts that make for unique and culturally significant souvenirs. The pieces are often inspired by traditional Greek patterns and techniques.

Kessaris Jewelry

Address: 10 Kolonaki Square, Athens 10673
Opening Hours: Monday to Friday, 10:00 AM – 8:00 PM; Saturday, 10:00 AM – 6:00 PM; Closed on Sundays

Kessaris is one of Athens' most renowned jewelry stores, known for its high-quality pieces and luxurious designs. The store offers a wide selection of fine jewelry, including both classic and contemporary styles. Kessaris is celebrated for its elegant creations and exceptional craftsmanship.

Highlights: The store's collection includes pieces featuring Greek motifs, including designs inspired by ancient Greek art and mythology. It's a great place to find sophisticated and timeless jewelry.

The Athens Art Gallery

Address: 38 Kolonaki Square, Athens 10673
Opening Hours: Monday to Friday, 10:00 AM – 8:00 PM; Saturday, 10:00 AM – 4:00 PM; Closed on Sundays

The Athens Art Gallery is a premier destination for contemporary Greek art. The gallery features a diverse collection of artworks by Greek artists, including paintings, sculptures, and mixed media pieces. It provides a platform for both emerging and established artists.

Highlights: The gallery's collection includes a range of artistic styles, from traditional to modern. It's an excellent place to purchase original Greek art and support local artists.

Diorite Art Gallery

Address: 11 Voukourestiou Street, Athens 10671
Opening Hours: Monday to Friday, 11:00 AM – 7:00 PM; Saturday, 11:00 AM – 3:00 PM; Closed on Sundays

Diorite Art Gallery specializes in contemporary art and offers a selection of works by both Greek and international artists. The gallery's focus is on innovative and thought-provoking pieces that push the boundaries of traditional art forms.

Highlights: Diorite Art Gallery is known for its high-quality exhibitions and diverse range of art. It's a great place to discover modern Greek art and find unique pieces for your collection.

The Benaki Museum Shop

Address: 1 Koumbari Street, Kolonaki, Athens 10674
Opening Hours: Monday to Saturday, 10:00 AM – 6:00 PM; Sunday, 10:00 AM – 3:00 PM

The Benaki Museum Shop offers a range of products inspired by Greek art and culture, including jewelry and decorative items. The shop features replicas of ancient artifacts, contemporary designs, and traditional crafts, providing a broad selection of high-quality items.

Highlights: The museum shop is known for its unique selection of handcrafted jewelry and art pieces, often reflecting themes from Greek history and mythology. It's an excellent place to find meaningful and artistic souvenirs.

Tips for Buying Jewelry and Art in Athens

Authenticity: Ensure that you are purchasing genuine Greek jewelry and art by buying from reputable stores and galleries.

Price Range: Greek jewelry and art come in a range of price points, so it's helpful to set a budget and explore options within your range.

Chapter Eight
Outdoor Activities And Entertainment

Coastal Walks and Beaches Near Athens

Athens, a city famed for its rich history and vibrant culture, also boasts stunning coastal landscapes that offer refreshing escapes from the urban hustle. The Athenian Riviera, stretching along the Saronic Gulf, features picturesque coastal walks and beautiful beaches that are perfect for relaxation and adventure.

Vouliagmeni Beach

Address: Vouliagmeni, Athens 16671
Opening Hours: Daily, 8:00 AM – 8:00 PM (seasonal)

Vouliagmeni Beach, located in the upscale suburb of Vouliagmeni, is renowned for its clear waters and well-maintained facilities. This organized beach offers a range of amenities, including sunbeds, umbrellas, and beachside cafés.

The calm, azure waters are perfect for swimming and water sports, making it a popular choice for both locals and visitors.

Highlights: The beach is ideal for families and those seeking a comfortable day by the sea. Its proximity to the Vouliagmeni Lake, known for its therapeutic hot springs, adds an extra layer of appeal. The lake is a short distance from the beach and provides a unique natural experience.

Glyfada Beach

Address: Glyfada, Athens 16674
Opening Hours: Daily, 8:00 AM – 9:00 PM (seasonal)

Glyfada Beach is a vibrant spot known for its lively atmosphere and array of dining and shopping options nearby. Located in the bustling neighborhood of Glyfada, this beach features well-kept facilities, including beach bars, restaurants, and water sports centers.

The sandy shores and clear waters make it an excellent place for a sun-soaked day out.

Highlights: The beach is close to Glyfada's shopping district, offering visitors the chance to explore local boutiques and enjoy a meal at one of the nearby restaurants. It's a great spot for those who enjoy combining beach time with urban amenities.

Cape Sounion

Address: Cape Sounion, Lavreotiki 19500
Opening Hours: Daily, 8:00 AM – 7:00 PM (varying hours depending on the season)

Cape Sounion, located about 70 kilometers southeast of Athens, is famous for its dramatic cliffs and the ancient Temple of Poseidon. While the area is more known for its historical site, it also offers stunning coastal walks and serene beaches nearby.

The Sounion Beach, situated in the vicinity, provides a more tranquil setting for relaxation and swimming.

Highlights: The coastal walk around Cape Sounion offers breathtaking views of the Aegean Sea and the iconic Temple of

Poseidon. Sunset views from this location are particularly spectacular, making it a must-visit spot for both history enthusiasts and nature lovers.

Lagonisi Beach

Address: Lagonisi, Athens 19010
Opening Hours: Daily, 9:00 AM – 7:00 PM (seasonal)

Lagonisi Beach, located in the southeastern suburbs of Athens, is known for its pristine waters and relaxed atmosphere. This beach is part of the Lagonisi Resort, offering a more private and upscale beach experience.

The clear waters and clean sandy shores make it a favorite among those looking for a more tranquil escape.

Highlights: The beach is ideal for a peaceful day by the sea, with facilities including sunbeds, umbrellas, and a beach bar. Its slightly secluded location ensures a less crowded experience compared to more central beaches.

Mikro and Mega Kavouri Beaches

Address: Vouliagmeni, Athens 16671
Opening Hours: Daily, 8:00 AM – 8:00 PM (seasonal)

Mikro and Mega Kavouri Beaches are two adjacent sandy stretches located in Vouliagmeni. Known for their clean, clear waters and relaxed atmosphere, these beaches are popular for swimming, sunbathing, and picnicking.

Both beaches are well-maintained and offer amenities such as sunbeds, umbrellas, and snack bars.

Highlights: The proximity of Mikro and Mega Kavouri Beaches allows visitors to explore both spots easily. The beaches are ideal for families and offer a range of activities, including beach volleyball and paddleboarding.

Schinias Beach

Address: Schinias, Marathon 19007
Opening Hours: Daily, 8:00 AM – 7:00 PM (seasonal)

Schinias Beach, located about 40 kilometers northeast of Athens, is renowned for its long sandy stretch and crystal-clear waters. The beach is part of the Schinias National Park, which also includes a lush pine forest.

This combination of natural beauty makes it a unique destination for beachgoers and nature enthusiasts alike.

Highlights: The beach's natural setting provides a picturesque backdrop for a day at the sea. The nearby forest offers opportunities for hiking and picnicking, making Schinias Beach a great spot for a full day of outdoor activities.

Varkiza Beach

Address: Varkiza, Athens 16672
Opening Hours: Daily, 8:00 AM – 8:00 PM (seasonal)

Varkiza Beach, situated in the southern suburbs of Athens, is a popular destination for its clean sandy shores and excellent facilities. The beach offers a range of amenities, including beach bars, restaurants, and water sports centers. Its well-organized setup makes it a comfortable spot for a day of relaxation.

Highlights: Varkiza Beach is known for its family-friendly atmosphere and well-maintained facilities. It's an excellent choice for those looking to enjoy a full day at the beach with all the necessary comforts.

Tips for Exploring Coastal Walks and Beaches

Transportation: Public transport options and taxis are available to most of these beaches, but renting a car can offer more flexibility, especially for exploring areas like Cape Sounion and Schinias.

Sun Protection: The Greek sun can be intense, so ensure you have sunscreen, a hat, and sunglasses.

Facilities: While some beaches offer extensive facilities, others may have more limited options. It's a good idea to bring essentials such as snacks, water, and beach towels.

Hiking Trails Around Mount Lycabettus and Philopappos Hill

Athens is not only a city of ancient history and vibrant culture but also a great destination for outdoor enthusiasts, offering several excellent hiking trails.

Mount Lycabettus and Philopappos Hill are two prominent landmarks that provide beautiful hiking opportunities and panoramic views of the city.

Mount Lycabettus

Address: Lycabettus Hill, Athens 11471
Opening Hours: Open daily, 24 hours

Mount Lycabettus, the highest point in central Athens, offers stunning views of the city and the surrounding landscape. The hill is accessible via several hiking trails, each providing a unique perspective of Athens.

Trail 1: Lycabettus Summit Trail

Distance: Approximately 1.5 kilometers (0.9 miles)

Duration: 30-45 minutes

Difficulty: Moderate

This popular trail starts from the base of the hill and winds its way up to the summit. The path is well-marked and paved, making it suitable for most hikers. Along the way, you'll encounter lush vegetation and various viewpoints that offer glimpses of Athens' landmarks, including the Acropolis.

Highlights: At the summit, you'll find the Saint George Chapel and an observation deck with panoramic views of Athens and the Aegean Sea. The trail is especially rewarding at sunset, when the city lights begin to twinkle.

Trail 2: The Alternative Trail from Kolonaki

Distance: Approximately 2 kilometers (1.2 miles)

Duration: 45-60 minutes

Difficulty: Moderate

This trail begins in the upscale Kolonaki neighborhood and ascends the hill from the eastern side. It's a less frequented path compared to the main trail, offering a quieter hiking experience. The trail is less paved and has some steeper sections, but it rewards hikers with varied terrain and beautiful views.

Highlights: The trail passes through residential areas and offers unique perspectives of Athens' architecture and green spaces. At the top, you can enjoy the same stunning views as from the main summit trail.

Philopappos Hill

Address: Philopappos Hill, Athens 11742
Opening Hours: Open daily, 24 hours

Philopappos Hill, also known as the Hill of the Muses, is famous for its historical monuments and scenic walking paths. The hill offers several trails that provide excellent views of Athens and its ancient sites.

Trail 1: The Philopappos Monument Trail

Distance: Approximately 1.2 kilometers (0.75 miles)

Duration: 30 minutes

Difficulty: Easy to Moderate

This trail takes you to the Philopappos Monument, a large mausoleum dedicated to Gaius Julius Antiochus Epiphanes Philopappos. The trail starts from the base of the hill and is relatively easy, with well-maintained paths and gentle inclines. It's a great option for a short hike with historical interest.

Highlights: The trail provides views of the monument and the surrounding landscape, including the Acropolis. The summit offers a panoramic view of the city and the surrounding hills, including a great vantage point for photography.

Trail 2: The Muses' Trail

Distance: Approximately 2 kilometers (1.2 miles)

Duration: 45 minutes

Difficulty: Moderate

This trail encircles the hill, passing through scenic spots and historical sites. The path is well-marked and includes sections of both paved and natural trails. It provides a more comprehensive exploration of the hill's natural beauty and historical significance.

Highlights: The trail offers varied views, including the ancient Agora, the Acropolis, and the city of Athens. It's a pleasant hike that combines history, nature, and great views.

Additional Tips for Hiking

Footwear: Wear comfortable hiking shoes or sturdy sneakers as some trails can be uneven or steep.

Water and Snacks: Bring water and snacks, especially if you plan to hike during the warmer months.

Weather: Check the weather forecast before heading out, as trails can be more challenging in rainy or hot conditions.

Maps and Signage: While trails are generally well-marked, carrying a map or GPS device can be helpful for navigation.

Nightclubs and Live Music Venues: Athens After Dark

Athens' vibrant nightlife scene is as diverse as the city itself, offering everything from high-energy nightclubs to intimate live music venues. Whether you're looking to dance the night away or enjoy live performances in a cozy setting, Athens has something for every night owl.

Lohan Nightclub

Address: 5-7 Valaoritou, Kolonaki, Athens 10671 **Opening Hours:** Wednesday to Saturday, 11:00 PM – 6:00 AM

Lohan Nightclub, co-owned by Lindsay Lohan, is a chic and upscale venue located in the heart of Kolonaki. Known for its stylish interior and top-notch DJs, Lohan offers a sophisticated atmosphere where you can dance to the latest electronic and house music.

The club also features impressive light shows and a well-stocked bar.

Highlights: The exclusive vibe and high-energy beats make it a hotspot for both locals and visitors looking for a glamorous night out. Be prepared for a lively crowd and an upscale dress code.

Six D.O.G.S

Address: 6-8 Avramiotou, Monastiraki, Athens 10551
Opening Hours: Daily, 8:00 PM – 3:00 AM

Six D.O.G.S is a popular multi-purpose venue in Monastiraki, offering a blend of live music, DJ sets, and art exhibitions. The space features a relaxed, alternative atmosphere with a focus on indie, electronic, and experimental music.

The venue includes an indoor stage and a courtyard, providing a versatile setting for various events.

Highlights: Six D.O.G.S is known for its eclectic programming and artsy ambiance. It's a great spot for discovering new music and enjoying a more laid-back night out.

Gagarin 205

Address: 205 Liosion Street, Athens 10445
Opening Hours: Event-dependent; typically evenings until late

Gagarin 205 is one of Athens' premier live music venues, hosting a diverse range of performances from rock and metal to electronic and hip-hop.

The venue is renowned for its excellent acoustics and dynamic atmosphere, making it a favorite among music enthusiasts.

Highlights: The venue's intimate setting allows for close-up experiences with performing artists. Check their schedule for upcoming shows and events.

Bios

Address: 84 Pireos Street, Kerameikos, Athens 11854
Opening Hours: Daily, 8:00 PM – 3:00 AM

Bios is a contemporary cultural space in Kerameikos that combines a bar, restaurant, and performance space. Known for its innovative approach to live music and arts, Bios features performances by local and international artists, as well as DJ sets and art exhibitions. The venue's industrial-chic design adds to its unique atmosphere.

Highlights: The diverse range of performances and events ensures that there's always something interesting happening at Bios. It's a great place for those interested in experiencing cutting-edge music and art.

Rebetiki Stoa

Address: 17-19 Panagioti Tsaldari, Psiri, Athens 10554
Opening Hours: Daily, 8:00 PM – 2:00 AM

Rebetiki Stoa is a traditional Greek music venue in Psiri, specializing in rebetiko, a genre of Greek folk music. The venue offers an authentic experience with live performances featuring classic rebetiko tunes, as well as a selection of traditional Greek dishes and drinks.

Highlights: For a taste of traditional Greek music and culture, Rebetiki Stoa offers an intimate and nostalgic experience. It's a perfect spot for those wanting to explore Greece's musical heritage.

Lido Bar

Address: 10 Kifisias Avenue, Kolonaki, Athens 10675
Opening Hours: Daily, 9:00 PM – 4:00 AM

Lido Bar, located in the upscale Kolonaki district, offers a sophisticated nightlife experience with an emphasis on classic cocktails and elegant decor. The venue features a mix of live music and DJ sets, with a focus on jazz, soul, and lounge music.

Highlights: The chic ambiance and stylish crowd make Lido Bar an ideal spot for a more refined night out. The venue's selection of cocktails and fine spirits enhances the upscale atmosphere.

Stavros Niarchos Foundation Cultural Center (SNFCC) - Summer Festival

Address: 364 Syngrou Avenue, Kallithea, Athens 17674
Opening Hours: Seasonal; typically evening events

While not a nightclub, the SNFCC's summer festival offers a range of live performances and cultural events in a stunning outdoor setting. The venue hosts concerts, theater performances, and dance shows during the warmer months, providing a unique way to enjoy Athens' cultural scene.

Highlights: The outdoor amphitheater and the stunning views of the surrounding park create a memorable setting for live performances. It's a great option for enjoying music and culture under the stars.

Tips for Enjoying Athens' Nightlife

Reservations: Some venues, especially high-end nightclubs and popular live music spots, may require reservations or have an entry fee.

Dress Code: Many nightclubs and upscale bars have dress codes, so it's a good idea to check ahead and dress accordingly.

Public Transport: Athens' nightlife areas are generally well-served by public transport, but consider using a taxi or rideshare service if you're out late.

Safety: As with any city, be mindful of your belongings and stay aware of your surroundings while enjoying Athens' nightlife.

Open-Air Cinemas: A Greek Summer Tradition

As the summer sun sets over Athens, a unique tradition comes alive: open-air cinemas. These charming venues, nestled in the heart of the city and its suburbs, offer a nostalgic and enchanting way to experience films under the starry sky.

Cine Thisio

Address: 7 Dionysiou Areopagitou Street, Athens 11742
Opening Hours: Daily, 8:30 PM – 12:00 AM (Seasonal)

Cine Thisio is one of the most iconic open-air cinemas in Athens, offering breathtaking views of the Acropolis while you enjoy your film. Located in the historic neighborhood of Thisio, this cinema has been serving moviegoers since 1935.

The ambiance is enhanced by the beautiful setting and the backdrop of the ancient ruins.

Highlights: Cine Thisio is renowned for its romantic atmosphere and classic film screenings. The cinema's bar offers refreshments and traditional Greek snacks, making it a perfect spot for a relaxed evening.

Cine Paris

Address: 22 Kydathineon Street, Plaka, Athens 10558
Opening Hours: Daily, 8:30 PM – 12:00 AM (Seasonal)

Cine Paris, located in the charming Plaka neighborhood, provides a delightful open-air movie experience with a view of the

Acropolis. The cinema, which opened in 1935, combines classic Greek cinema with contemporary films, offering a diverse selection of movies throughout the summer season.

Highlights: The intimate setting and historical surroundings create a unique movie-watching experience. The cinema's quaint bar serves a selection of drinks and snacks.

Cine Mavillis

Address: 24 Mavillias Street, Ampelokipi, Athens 11528
Opening Hours: Daily, 8:30 PM – 12:00 AM (Seasonal)

Cine Mavillis is a beloved open-air cinema located in the Ampelokipi area. Known for its cozy atmosphere and friendly staff, it provides a great setting for enjoying films with a local flavor.

The cinema features a mix of Greek and international films and is popular among both locals and visitors.

Highlights: The relaxed vibe and affordable tickets make Cine Mavillis a favorite among budget-conscious moviegoers. It's an excellent choice for a casual night out.

Cine Zefyros

Address: 4 Iera Odos Street, Kerameikos, Athens 10435
Opening Hours: Daily, 8:30 PM – 12:00 AM (Seasonal)

Cine Zefyros, located in the vibrant Kerameikos neighborhood, is known for its eclectic programming and laid-back atmosphere. The cinema offers a range of films, from classic Greek cinema to contemporary international hits.

The open-air setting adds a charming touch to the movie-watching experience.

Highlights: Cine Zefyros often hosts special events and themed nights, making it a lively and engaging place to catch a film. The cinema's outdoor bar serves drinks and snacks.

Cine Aegli

Address: 5 Panepistimiou Street, Omonia, Athens 10671
Opening Hours: Daily, 8:30 PM – 12:00 AM (Seasonal)

Cine Aegli, located in the bustling Omonia area, offers a classic open-air cinema experience with a focus on quality film programming.

The cinema's central location makes it easily accessible, and its outdoor setting provides a pleasant escape from the city's hustle and bustle.

Highlights: The cinema's large screen and comfortable seating ensure a great viewing experience. Cine Aegli also features a selection of refreshments and snacks.

Tips for Enjoying Open-Air Cinemas

Arrive Early: To secure a good seat, especially during peak summer months, it's a good idea to arrive a bit early.

Dress Comfortably: Evenings in Athens can be cool, so bring a light jacket or sweater.

Bring Cash: Some open-air cinemas may not accept credit cards, so it's wise to have cash on hand for tickets and refreshments.

Chapter Nine

Accommodations in Athens

Luxury Hotels with Acropolis Views

Athens, a city renowned for its rich history and vibrant culture, offers some of the most breathtaking luxury accommodations with views of the iconic Acropolis.

Staying in a hotel with an Acropolis view not only provides a unique perspective of the city's ancient landmarks but also adds a touch of elegance and comfort to your visit.

Hotel Grande Bretagne

Address: 1 Vasileos Georgiou A' Street, Syntagma Square, Athens 10564
Opening Hours: 24 hours

Hotel Grande Bretagne, an iconic five-star hotel, stands majestically in Syntagma Square and offers unparalleled views of the Acropolis from many of its rooms and suites. Known for its opulent decor and impeccable service, this historic hotel combines classical elegance with modern luxury.

Highlights: The hotel's rooftop restaurant, "GB Roof Garden," provides panoramic views of the Acropolis, especially enchanting at sunset.

The hotel also features a spa, a state-of-the-art fitness center, and exquisite dining options. Its prime location places it close to major attractions, shopping, and dining.

King George Hotel

Address: 3 Vasileos Georgiou A' Street, Syntagma Square, Athens 10564
Opening Hours: 24 hours

Part of the Luxury Collection, King George Hotel offers a sophisticated blend of historic charm and modern luxury. Located adjacent to Syntagma Square, the hotel provides magnificent views of the Acropolis from its elegant rooms and suites.

The hotel's design is a nod to its storied past, featuring classic European decor and high-end amenities.

Highlights: The "King George Restaurant," located on the rooftop, offers an exquisite dining experience with stunning views of the Acropolis and the city skyline. The hotel also boasts a well-equipped fitness center and offers personalized concierge services to enhance your stay.

Electra Metropolis

Address: 15 Mitropoleos Street, Syntagma, Athens 10557
Opening Hours: 24 hours

Electra Metropolis, a modern luxury hotel located in the heart of Athens, offers contemporary elegance with magnificent views of the Acropolis. The hotel's design blends sleek modernity with classic touches, providing a comfortable and stylish base for exploring the city.

Highlights: The rooftop restaurant, "Metropolis Roof Garden," offers a spectacular dining experience with panoramic views of the Acropolis and the city.

The hotel also features a luxurious spa, an outdoor pool, and a fully-equipped fitness center. Its central location makes it convenient for sightseeing and shopping.

St. George Lycabettus Boutique Hotel

Address: 2 Kleomenous Street, Kolonaki, Athens 10675
Opening Hours: 24 hours

Perched on the slopes of Mount Lycabettus, St. George Lycabettus Boutique Hotel offers stunning views of the Acropolis and the city from its rooms and suites. Known for its contemporary design and exceptional service, this boutique hotel combines luxury with a warm, welcoming atmosphere.

Highlights: The hotel's rooftop restaurant, "La Suite Lounge," provides an intimate setting with breathtaking views of the Acropolis and the cityscape. The hotel also features a wellness center, an outdoor pool, and stylishly designed rooms with modern amenities.

New Hotel

Address: 16 Filellinon Street, Syntagma, Athens 10557
Opening Hours: 24 hours

New Hotel is a chic and modern luxury accommodation that offers stunning views of the Acropolis. Designed by renowned architects and designers, the hotel combines cutting-edge design with comfort and sophistication.

Located near Syntagma Square, it provides easy access to major attractions.

Highlights: The hotel's rooftop terrace offers a beautiful setting for dining and relaxation with views of the Acropolis. New Hotel features a contemporary restaurant, a fully-equipped gym, and stylish rooms with unique decor and modern amenities.

AthensWas Hotel

Address: 5 Dionysiou Areopagitou Street, Athens 11742
Opening Hours: 24 hours

AthensWas Hotel is a luxurious boutique hotel located near the Acropolis Museum. The hotel's modern design and high-end amenities make it a perfect choice for those looking to stay close to the ancient sites while enjoying luxurious comfort. Many rooms offer unobstructed views of the Acropolis.

Highlights: The hotel's rooftop bar, "Athenian Stoa," offers stunning views of the Acropolis and a sophisticated ambiance for enjoying drinks and light meals. The hotel also provides personalized service, a contemporary fitness center, and stylish rooms with modern comforts.

Tips for Choosing a Luxury Hotel with Acropolis Views

Book Early: Luxury hotels with Acropolis views are highly sought after, so it's advisable to book well in advance to secure your preferred room type and view.

Check Room Categories: Some hotels offer specific room categories with guaranteed Acropolis views, so be sure to inquire about this when booking.

Consider Dining Options: Many of these hotels have rooftop restaurants or bars with Acropolis views, making it a great option to enjoy meals with a spectacular backdrop.

Review Seasonal Offers: Check for any special offers or packages that might include additional perks such as guided tours or spa treatments.

Mid-Range and Boutique Hotels

Athens' mid-range and boutique hotels offer a blend of style, comfort, and affordability. These accommodations provide a personalized experience, often with unique decor and thoughtful amenities, making them ideal for travelers who want to enjoy the city's charm without breaking the bank.

Hotel Ergon

Address: 23 Karaiskaki Street, Monastiraki, Athens 10554
Opening Hours: 24 hours

Hotel Ergon is a stylish boutique hotel located in the vibrant Monastiraki district, known for its bustling markets and proximity to major attractions. The hotel offers contemporary rooms with modern amenities, reflecting a sleek and minimalist design. It's an excellent choice for travelers seeking both comfort and convenience.

Highlights: The hotel features a rooftop terrace with views of the Acropolis, perfect for enjoying breakfast or a drink. Its central location provides easy access to the city's landmarks, shopping, and dining options.

Art Hotel Athens

Address: 29-31 Agias Irinis Square, Plaka, Athens 10560
Opening Hours: 24 hours

Art Hotel Athens is located in the historic Plaka neighborhood, offering a blend of modern design and artistic flair. The hotel is known for its unique decor, featuring contemporary art and stylish furnishings. Its location provides easy access to popular sites like the Acropolis and the Ancient Agora.

Highlights: The hotel's breakfast buffet includes a selection of local and international dishes. The friendly staff and artistic ambiance create a welcoming atmosphere for guests.

Kimon Athens Hotel

Address: 6 Agion Assomaton Street, Plaka, Athens 10554
Opening Hours: 24 hours

Kimon Athens Hotel is a charming boutique hotel situated in the picturesque Plaka area. The hotel offers comfortable and well-appointed rooms with traditional Greek decor.

Its central location is ideal for exploring Athens' historic sites, shops, and restaurants.

Highlights: The hotel features a cozy lounge area and a complimentary breakfast with a selection of Greek and international options. The attentive staff and quaint atmosphere enhance the guest experience.

Athens Gate Hotel

Address: 10 Syngrou Avenue, Athens 11742
Opening Hours: 24 hours

Athens Gate Hotel is a modern mid-range hotel located near the Acropolis Museum and Temple of Olympian Zeus. The hotel offers comfortable rooms with contemporary furnishings and excellent views of the Acropolis from its upper floors and rooftop restaurant.

Highlights: The rooftop restaurant provides a stunning panoramic view of the Acropolis, especially at sunset. The hotel's location is ideal for sightseeing, with major attractions just a short walk away.

Mosaico Suites

Address: 21 Panagioti Tsaldari Street, Psiri, Athens 10554
Opening Hours: 24 hours

Mosaico Suites offers a blend of modern comfort and artistic design in the lively Psiri district. The hotel features stylish suites with contemporary decor and high-end amenities. Its location is convenient for exploring Athens' vibrant nightlife and cultural attractions.

Highlights: The hotel's design emphasizes local artwork and modern aesthetics. Guests can enjoy a comfortable stay with easy access to nearby restaurants and bars.

New Art Hotel

Address: 16 Filellinon Street, Syntagma, Athens 10557
Opening Hours: 24 hours

New Art Hotel is a contemporary boutique hotel located in Syntagma, close to major landmarks and shopping areas. The hotel features modern rooms with sleek decor and high-tech amenities. Its central location makes it a great base for exploring Athens.

Highlights: The hotel offers a stylish lobby, a fitness center, and a buffet breakfast. The modern design and convenient location make it a popular choice for travelers.

Coco-Mat Hotel Athens

Address: 36 Vasilissis Sofias Avenue, Athens 10676
Opening Hours: 24 hours

Coco-Mat Hotel Athens is known for its eco-friendly approach and focus on sustainability. Located near the Athens Concert Hall, the hotel offers comfortable rooms with natural materials and a contemporary design. It's a great choice for eco-conscious travelers seeking a comfortable and stylish stay.

Highlights: The hotel features a unique design with a focus on natural elements. Guests can enjoy a healthy breakfast and relax in the serene atmosphere of the hotel's rooms and common areas.

Tips for Choosing Mid-Range and Boutique Hotels

Check for Special Offers: Many boutique hotels offer seasonal promotions or packages that include additional perks like guided tours or dining credits.

Location Matters: Consider the hotel's proximity to major attractions, public transport, and dining options to enhance your stay.

Read Reviews: Look for recent guest reviews to get an idea of the hotel's service quality and any potential issues.

Amenities: Verify the amenities offered, such as Wi-Fi, breakfast, and room comfort, to ensure they meet your needs.

Budget-Friendly Hostels and Guesthouses

For travelers looking to explore Athens on a budget, the city offers a range of hostels and guesthouses that provide both affordability and comfort.

These budget-friendly accommodations are perfect for backpackers, solo travelers, and those seeking a more economical stay without compromising on quality.

City Circus Athens

Address: 16, Lempesi Street, Psiri, Athens 10554
Opening Hours: 24 hours

City Circus Athens is a highly-rated hostel located in the vibrant Psiri district. It offers a unique, artistic vibe with comfortable dormitories and private rooms. The hostel's design features colorful murals and eclectic decor, reflecting the lively spirit of Athens.

Highlights: City Circus offers free Wi-Fi, a communal kitchen, and a lounge area for guests to relax. The hostel also organizes social events and city tours, making it a great place to meet other travelers. Its central location provides easy access to major attractions and nightlife.

Athens Backpackers

Address: 12 Makri Street, Plaka, Athens 10555
Opening Hours: 24 hours

Athens Backpackers is a popular hostel situated in the historic Plaka neighborhood. Known for its friendly atmosphere and clean facilities, the hostel offers both dormitory and private room options. It's conveniently located near the Acropolis and other major sites.

Highlights: The hostel features a rooftop bar with panoramic views of the Acropolis, a communal kitchen, and organized events. Free Wi-Fi and daily breakfast are included, adding value to your stay. Its proximity to historical landmarks and local eateries makes it a practical choice.

Stefanos Hostel

Address: 10, Agiou Konstantinou Street, Omonia, Athens 10431
Opening Hours: 24 hours

Stefanos Hostel provides a budget-friendly option in the central Omonia area. The hostel offers simple yet comfortable dormitory-style accommodation with essential amenities. It's ideal for travelers seeking basic but clean and affordable lodging.

Highlights: Stefanos Hostel offers free Wi-Fi, a 24-hour reception, and a communal kitchen. Its central location provides easy access to public transportation and key attractions. The hostel's straightforward approach ensures a hassle-free stay.

Pella Inn Hostel

Address: 104 Pireos Street, Psiri, Athens 10553
Opening Hours: 24 hours

Pella Inn Hostel is a modern and budget-friendly hostel located in the bustling Psiri district. The hostel features clean and comfortable rooms with a contemporary design. It's a great choice for travelers who want to be close to the city's vibrant nightlife and cultural sites.

Highlights: The hostel offers free Wi-Fi, a shared kitchen, and a lounge area. Guests can enjoy a complimentary breakfast and take advantage of the hostel's proximity to local restaurants and bars. Its location also provides easy access to historical landmarks.

Kimon Hotel

Address: 6 Agion Assomaton Street, Plaka, Athens 10554
Opening Hours: 24 hours

Kimon Hotel is a charming guesthouse situated in the picturesque Plaka neighborhood. Offering budget-friendly accommodation with a homely atmosphere, it's ideal for those looking for a comfortable and affordable stay in a historic setting.

Highlights: The guesthouse provides basic amenities, including free Wi-Fi, a communal kitchen, and a shared lounge. The location allows guests to explore Athens on foot, with major attractions and local eateries nearby.

Its welcoming environment and central location make it a popular choice for budget travelers.

Hostel Zeus

Address: 3, Kydathineon Street, Plaka, Athens 10558
Opening Hours: 24 hours

Hostel Zeus is a budget-friendly option located in the heart of Plaka, close to the Acropolis and other major attractions. The hostel offers a range of dormitory and private room accommodations with essential amenities and a relaxed atmosphere.

Highlights: The hostel features free Wi-Fi, a communal kitchen, and a cozy common area. Guests can enjoy a complimentary breakfast and explore the nearby historic sites and local shops. The central location and friendly staff make it a convenient and pleasant choice for travelers.

Zorbas Hostel

Address: 37-39, Kifissias Avenue, Kolonaki, Athens 10673
Opening Hours: 24 hours

Zorbas Hostel is located in the upscale Kolonaki area, offering budget accommodation with a touch of elegance. The hostel provides simple but comfortable rooms with modern amenities, making it a good option for those who want to stay in a more refined neighborhood.

Highlights: Zorbas Hostel offers free Wi-Fi, a shared kitchen, and a lounge area. Its location in Kolonaki provides easy access to upscale dining and shopping, while still being close to public transport for exploring the city.

Tips for Choosing Budget-Friendly Hostels and Guesthouses

Check Reviews: Read recent guest reviews to ensure the hostel or guesthouse meets your expectations for cleanliness, comfort, and service.

Consider Location: Choose accommodations that are conveniently located near public transportation and major attractions to save time and money.

Look for Extras: Some hostels and guesthouses offer additional perks such as free breakfast, organized tours, or social events, which can enhance your stay.

Book in Advance: Budget accommodations can fill up quickly, especially during peak travel seasons, so booking in advance can help secure the best rates and availability.

Chapter Ten
Practical Information

Currency, ATMs, and Banking in Athens

Navigating the currency, ATMs, and banking services in Athens is straightforward, making it easy for travelers to manage their finances while exploring the city.

Currency

The official currency of Greece is the Euro (€). As a member of the Eurozone, Greece uses the Euro for all transactions, and you will find it widely accepted across Athens. The Euro is divided into 100 cents, and banknotes come in denominations of €5, €10, €20, €50, €100, €200, and €500. Coins are available in denominations of 1, 2, 5, 10, 20, and 50 cents, and €1 and €2.

ATMs

ATMs are readily available throughout Athens, providing easy access to cash. Most ATMs accept international credit and debit cards, including Visa, Mastercard, and American Express.

The typical withdrawal limit is around €200 to €500 per transaction, though this can vary by bank and card issuer. ATMs are commonly found in central areas, near tourist attractions, and within major shopping districts.

Notable ATM Locations:

Bank of Greece ATM
Address: 3 Stadiou Street, Syntagma, Athens 10562
Opening Hours: 24 hours
Located near Syntagma Square, this ATM is centrally situated and provides convenient access to cash for travelers exploring the area. The Bank of Greece is the country's central bank and offers reliable ATM services.

National Bank of Greece ATM
Address: 87-89 Stadiou Street, Syntagma, Athens 10559
Opening Hours: 24 hours
This ATM is positioned in the heart of Athens, close to major landmarks and shopping areas. The National Bank of Greece is one of the largest banks in the country, ensuring secure and efficient transactions.

Alpha Bank ATM
Address: 40 Panepistimiou Street, Athens 10679
Opening Hours: 24 hours
Situated near the main commercial district, this ATM offers easy access for visitors exploring Athens' bustling shopping streets and nearby attractions.

Banking Services

Banking services in Athens are accessible and efficient, with numerous branches of both Greek and international banks throughout the city. Most banks are open Monday to Friday from 8:00 AM to 2:30 PM. Many branches close on weekends, but ATMs remain operational around the clock.

Notable Banks and Their Addresses:

National Bank of Greece
Address: 87-89 Stadiou Street, Syntagma, Athens 10559
Opening Hours: Monday to Friday, 8:00 AM to 2:30 PM
Website: www.nbg.gr
As one of Greece's largest and oldest banks, National Bank of Greece offers a wide range of banking services, including currency exchange, account management, and financial advice.

Alpha Bank
Address: 40 Panepistimiou Street, Athens 10679
Opening Hours: Monday to Friday, 8:00 AM to 2:30 PM
Website: www.alpha.gr
Alpha Bank provides comprehensive banking services and is well-regarded for its customer service. The bank offers foreign exchange services, ATM access, and personal banking.

Eurobank
Address: 8 Souri Street, Kolonaki, Athens 10673
Opening Hours: Monday to Friday, 8:00 AM to 2:30 PM
Website: www.eurobank.gr
Eurobank is another prominent bank in Athens, offering a full suite of banking services, including ATMs and customer support for both locals and travelers.

Piraeus Bank
Address: 4-6 Tzavella Street, Exarchia, Athens 10683
Opening Hours: Monday to Friday, 8:00 AM to 2:30 PM
Website: www.piraeusbank.gr
Known for its extensive network of branches and ATMs, Piraeus Bank offers a range of banking services including currency exchange and international banking.

Tips for Managing Money in Athens

Currency Exchange: While many ATMs offer competitive exchange rates, you might also find currency exchange services at banks, post offices, and dedicated exchange offices. Compare rates to get the best deal.

Notify Your Bank: Before traveling, inform your bank of your travel plans to avoid any issues with using your card abroad. This helps prevent your card from being flagged for suspicious activity.

Keep Small Cash Handy: While credit and debit cards are widely accepted, carrying some cash for smaller purchases or places that do not accept cards is advisable.

Language Tips and Common Greek Phrases

While many people in Athens speak English, especially in tourist areas, knowing a few basic Greek phrases can enhance your experience and show respect for the local culture.

Language Tips

Basic Pronunciation: Greek pronunciation can be quite different from English. Familiarize yourself with the Greek alphabet and some common sounds to help with pronunciation. For example, "χ" (chi) is pronounced like the "ch" in "Bach," and "θ" (theta) is pronounced like the "th" in "think."

Politeness Matters: Greeks appreciate polite interactions. Using basic greetings and expressions of gratitude will go a long way in making a positive impression.

English is Widely Spoken: In tourist areas, hotels, restaurants, and shops, many people speak English. However, using Greek phrases can be helpful and appreciated.

Learn the Numbers: Knowing basic numbers will help with understanding prices, directions, and other numerical information.

Practice Phrases: Practice a few key phrases before your trip. Even a small effort to speak Greek can be warmly received by locals.

Common Greek Phrases

Here are some essential Greek phrases that will be useful during your travels in Athens:

Greetings and Introductions:

Hello: Γειά σας (Yia sas) *Formal or plural; for informal use, simply say Γειά (Yia).*

Goodbye: Αντίο (Adio)

Good morning: Καλημέρα (Kalimera)

Good evening: Καλησπέρα (Kalispéra)

Good night: Καληνύχτα (Kalinychta)

How are you?: Πώς είστε; (Pos íste?)
Formal or plural; for informal use, say Πώς είσαι; (Pos íse?)

Polite Expressions:

Please: Παρακαλώ (Parakaló)

Thank you: Ευχαριστώ (Efcharistó)

You're welcome: Παρακαλώ (Parakaló) or Με τίποτα (Me típota)

Excuse me / Sorry: Συγγνώμη (Signómi)

Basic Questions:

Do you speak English?: Μιλάτε Αγγλικά; (Miláte Angliká?)

Where is...?: Πού είναι...; (Poú eínai...?)
For example, Πού είναι η τουαλέτα; (Poú eínai i toualéta?) – Where is the bathroom?

How much does it cost?: Πόσο κοστίζει; (Póso kostízi?)

What time is it?: Τι ώρα είναι; (Ti óra eínai?)

Can I get the bill?: Μπορώ να έχω τον λογαριασμό; (Boró na écho ton logariasmó?)

Food and Dining:

Menu: Μενού (Menoú)

I would like…: Θα ήθελα... (Tha íthela...)
For example, Θα ήθελα ένα καφέ (Tha íthela ena kafé) – I would like a coffee.

Water: Νερό (Neró)

Wine: Κρασί (Krasí)

Travel and Directions:

How do I get to…?: Πώς πάω στο...; (Pós páo sto...?)
For example, Πώς πάω στο Σύνταγμα; (Pós páo sto Síndagma?) – How do I get to Syntagma?

Left: Αριστερά (Aristerá)

Right: Δεξιά (Dexiá)

Straight ahead: Ευθεία (Efthía)

Emergency Phrases:

Help!: Βοήθεια! (Voítheia!)

Call the police!: Καλέστε την αστυνομία! (Kaleté tin astynomía!)

I need a doctor: Χρειάζομαι γιατρό (Chreiázomai giatró)

Tips for Using Greek Phrases

Practice Pronunciation: Use language apps or online resources to practice pronunciation and listen to native speakers.

Be Patient: If you're not sure how to pronounce something, don't hesitate to ask for help or use a translation app.

Engage with Locals: Don't be afraid to use Greek phrases even if you're not perfect. Locals will appreciate your effort and often respond in English if needed.

Wi-Fi, Mobile Connectivity, and Sim Cards

Staying connected while traveling is crucial, and Athens offers a range of options for Wi-Fi, mobile connectivity, and SIM cards.

Wi-Fi

Free Public Wi-Fi: Athens provides several free public Wi-Fi hotspots, especially in tourist areas and public spaces. You can access free Wi-Fi at:

Syntagma Square: Free Wi-Fi is available around Syntagma Square, a central hub near major attractions and public transport.

Monastiraki Square: Another popular area with free public Wi-Fi, ideal for checking maps and staying connected while exploring.

Public Parks: Many public parks and squares, such as the National Garden of Athens, offer free Wi-Fi.

Cafés and Restaurants: Most cafés, restaurants, and bars in Athens offer free Wi-Fi to their patrons. Popular spots include:

Taf   **Café**
Address: 12 Normanou Street, Monastiraki, Athens 10555
Opening Hours: Daily from 10:00 AM to 2:00 AM
Known for its relaxed atmosphere, Taf Café provides free Wi-Fi for customers.

Kiki   **de**   **Grèce**
Address: 24 Karyatidon Street, Plaka, Athens 10558
Opening Hours: Daily from 9:00 AM to 9:00 PM
This cozy café offers free Wi-Fi along with its delicious coffee and pastries.

Accommodation:
Most hotels, hostels, and guesthouses in Athens offer free Wi-Fi to guests. Check with your accommodation before booking to ensure that Wi-Fi is included in the room rate.

Mobile Connectivity

Mobile   **Networks:**
Greece has several mobile network providers offering robust coverage across Athens. The major providers include:

COSMOTE: One of the largest and most reliable networks, offering extensive coverage and competitive data plans.

Vodafone Greece: Provides strong coverage and various prepaid and postpaid options.

Wind: Known for affordable plans and good coverage, particularly in urban areas.

International Roaming:
If you're traveling with an international mobile plan, check with your carrier about roaming charges and data packages. Many international carriers offer roaming services in Greece, but costs can vary.

Local SIM Cards:
For affordable and flexible connectivity, consider purchasing a local SIM card. Here's how you can get one:

Airport Kiosks: SIM cards are available at kiosks in Athens International Airport. Look for providers like COSMOTE, Vodafone, and Wind.

Mobile Network Stores: You can buy SIM cards at network provider stores throughout Athens. Examples include:

COSMOTE Store
Address: 9 Ermou Street, Syntagma, Athens 10563
Opening Hours: Monday to Friday, 9:00 AM to 5:00 PM; Saturday, 9:00 AM to 3:00 PM

Vodafone Store
Address: 14 Stadiou Street, Syntagma, Athens 10559
Opening Hours: Monday to Friday, 9:00 AM to 5:00 PM; Saturday, 9:00 AM to 3:00 PM

Wind Store
Address: 32 Panepistimiou Street, Athens 10679
Opening Hours: Monday to Friday, 9:00 AM to 5:00 PM; Saturday, 9:00 AM to 3:00 PM

Prepaid   SIM   Cards:
Prepaid SIM cards are a convenient option for short-term visitors. They come with various data packages and can be topped up as needed. Packages typically include a combination of call minutes, texts, and data.

Documentation:
To purchase a SIM card, you'll need to present your passport or ID. This is a standard requirement for activating a local SIM in Greece.

Tips for Staying Connected

Compare Plans: Check different providers for the best rates and data packages that suit your needs.

Check Coverage: Ensure the provider offers good coverage in the areas you plan to visit.

Wi-Fi Security: When using public Wi-Fi, be cautious about security. Avoid accessing sensitive information or making financial transactions on unsecured networks.

Emergency Numbers and Health Services

Navigating emergency situations and accessing health services is crucial when traveling. Athens, as a bustling metropolis, offers robust emergency and healthcare services to ensure the safety and well-being of its residents and visitors.

Emergency Numbers

Police - 100

For immediate assistance from the police, dial 100. This number is essential for reporting crimes, accidents, or other urgent situations requiring police intervention.

The Greek police are well-trained and responsive, and they can assist with various issues ranging from theft and vandalism to accidents and disturbances. The service is available 24/7.

Ambulance - 166

For medical emergencies, including severe injuries, sudden illnesses, or accidents requiring urgent medical care, call 166. Greek ambulances are equipped with advanced medical technology and staffed by highly trained paramedics who provide prompt care. This number ensures quick access to emergency medical services across the city.

Fire Department - 199

In the event of a fire or other fire-related emergencies, such as chemical spills or rescues, dial 199. The fire department in Athens is skilled in handling various emergencies, from small fires to large-scale disasters. Their quick response is crucial for minimizing damage and ensuring safety.

General Emergency Services - 112

The European Union emergency number 112 can be dialed for police, medical, and fire emergencies. This number is useful for travelers who may not be fluent in Greek, as it operates in multiple languages and connects you with emergency services across the EU. It's a reliable alternative if you're unsure which service to contact.

Health Services

Athens boasts a comprehensive network of healthcare facilities, including public and private hospitals, clinics, and pharmacies, ensuring that medical needs are met effectively.

Public Hospitals

Attikon University Hospital: Located in Haidari, Attikon is a leading public hospital offering a wide range of medical services, including emergency care, specialized treatments, and surgeries.

Address: 1 Rimini Street, Haidari, Athens. Tel: +30 210 583 3000.

Evangelismos Hospital: Situated centrally, Evangelismos is one of the largest public hospitals in Greece, known for its extensive medical and surgical services. It also serves as a teaching hospital with advanced research facilities.

Address: 45-47 Vassileos Sofias Avenue, Athens. Tel: +30 210 72 89 100.

Private Hospitals

Hygeia Hospital: This prominent private hospital offers advanced healthcare services across various specialties. Hygeia is renowned for its modern facilities and high standard of care. Address: 4 Erythrou Stavrou Street, Marousi, Athens. Tel: +30 210 686 1000.

IASO Hospital: Known for its state-of-the-art medical technology and comprehensive care, IASO provides a wide range of medical services, including emergency care and specialized treatments.

Address: 38-40 Kifissias Avenue, Marousi, Athens. Tel: +30 210 618 8000.

Pharmacies

Pharmacies are plentiful in Athens, with many open 24/7 to meet urgent needs. You can find a list of open pharmacies through local directories or online. Look for signs labeled "φαρμακείο" (pharmacy) to locate them.

Pharmacies are crucial for obtaining medications, medical supplies, and advice on minor health issues.

Medical Clinics

Private Clinics: Numerous private clinics throughout Athens offer specialized medical care. Many clinics cater to international patients and provide services in English. These clinics cover a range of specialties, including general medicine, pediatrics, and dermatology.

Health Insurance

Travelers should ensure they have health insurance that covers medical emergencies abroad. Private hospitals and clinics may require payment upfront, so having comprehensive travel insurance with emergency medical coverage is essential.

Keep a copy of your insurance policy and contact details for quick reference.

Practical Tips

Language: While many medical professionals in Athens speak English, having a translation app or understanding basic Greek medical terms can be beneficial.

Prescriptions: Carry a copy of any prescriptions or a doctor's note to facilitate obtaining necessary medications at local pharmacies.

Health Precautions: Stay hydrated, be cautious with street food, and use insect repellent to avoid mosquito-borne illnesses.

Chapter Eleven
Resources for Travelers

Recommended Apps for Exploring Athens

Exploring Athens can be greatly enhanced with the help of various mobile apps designed to make your travel experience smoother and more enjoyable. Here are some highly recommended apps for discovering Athens:

Google Maps

Purpose: Navigation, local business information, and route planning.

Features: Provides detailed maps, real-time traffic updates, and walking, driving, or public transit directions. You can also find reviews and contact details for local businesses and attractions.

TripAdvisor

Purpose: Reviews and recommendations for restaurants, attractions, and accommodations.

Features: Offers user reviews, photos, and ratings for a wide range of dining options, attractions, and hotels. It also provides booking options and personalized recommendations based on your interests.

Athens Travel Guide by Triposo

Purpose: Comprehensive travel guide for Athens.

Features: Offline maps, detailed descriptions of attractions, local tips, and recommendations. It covers major sights, restaurants, and cultural highlights, helping you plan your itinerary.

Citymapper

Purpose: Public transportation planning and navigation.

Features: Offers detailed public transit information, including bus, metro, and tram routes. It provides real-time updates and helps you find the quickest routes around Athens.

Eventbrite

Purpose: Finding and booking local events and activities.

Features: Lists local events, festivals, and activities happening in Athens. You can browse events by category, date, and location, and purchase tickets directly through the app.

XE Currency

Purpose: Currency conversion and exchange rate information.

Features: Provides up-to-date exchange rates and currency conversion tools, which is helpful for budgeting and making transactions in different currencies.

GreekPod101

Purpose: Learning basic Greek phrases and language.

Features: Offers language lessons, pronunciation guides, and useful phrases for navigating daily interactions in Greece. It's useful for communicating with locals and understanding cultural nuances.

Athens Metro Map

Purpose: Metro system navigation.

Features: Provides a detailed map of the Athens Metro system, including station information and route planning. Essential for navigating Athens' extensive metro network efficiently.

GetYourGuide

Purpose: Booking tours and activities.

Features: Lists and allows you to book various tours, excursions, and activities in Athens. Includes options for guided tours, skip-the-line tickets, and unique experiences.

Kompass

Purpose: Detailed local maps and points of interest.

Features: Offers offline maps with detailed points of interest, including landmarks, restaurants, and attractions. Useful for exploring Athens without relying on mobile data.

Maps.me

Purpose: Offline maps and navigation.

Features: Provides detailed offline maps with GPS navigation. Ideal for exploring Athens without an internet connection, allowing you to navigate and discover places with ease.

Key Websites and Visitor Information Centers

Websites

Visit Athens

Website: visit.athens

Description: The official tourism website for Athens, offering detailed information on attractions, dining, shopping, and accommodations. It includes useful tips, suggested itineraries, and updates on local events.

Athens Guide

Website: athensguide.com

Description: A comprehensive guide to Athens with information on historical sites, museums, restaurants, and entertainment. It provides practical travel tips, local news, and recommendations.

Greek Tourism Organization

Website: gnto.gr

Description: The official site of the Greek National Tourism Organization, offering information on travel destinations across Greece, including Athens. It includes details on accommodation, transportation, and cultural experiences.

TripAdvisor Athens

Website: tripadvisor.com

Description: Provides reviews, ratings, and recommendations for Athens' attractions, restaurants, and hotels. It also features user-generated content and booking options.

Lonely Planet Athens

Website: lonelyplanet.com

Description: Offers travel guides, tips, and insights into Athens. The site includes top sights, local experiences, and practical advice for travelers.

Visitor Information Centers

Athens Tourist Information Center

Location: Syntagma Square, Athens (near the Syntagma Metro Station)

Description: The main visitor information center in Athens, providing brochures, maps, and assistance with local attractions and services. Staff offer guidance on tours, transportation, and accommodation.

Athens City Hall Tourist Information

Location: 1 Kallidromiou Street, Athens

Description: Located in City Hall, this center offers tourist information, including local maps, event information, and general advice about exploring Athens.

Acropolis Museum Visitor Center

Location: 15 Dionysiou Areopagitou Street, Athens

Description: Located at the Acropolis Museum, this center provides information about the museum, guided tours, and nearby attractions. It's a useful starting point if you're visiting the Acropolis area.

Piraeus Port Tourist Information

Location: Piraeus Port, Athens

Description: For travelers arriving by ferry, this center offers information on transportation, local services, and connections to Athens city center.

Omonia Square Tourist Information Center

Location: Omonia Square, Athens

Description: Located in the central area of Athens, this center provides maps, brochures, and general tourist information.

Athens' Tourist Cards and Passes for Attractions

Athens offers several tourist cards and passes that can enhance your sightseeing experience, providing convenience and potential savings on entry fees to major attractions. Here's to the most popular options:

Athens City Pass

Overview: The Athens City Pass offers a range of options including access to major tourist sites and public transport.

Features:

Athens City Pass Basic: Includes free entry to popular sites like the Acropolis Museum and the Ancient Agora, along with a hop-on, hop-off bus tour. It often includes a guidebook and map.

Athens City Pass Premium: Provides access to a broader range of attractions, including skip-the-line access at popular sites, and may include additional perks such as guided tours or dining discounts.

Where to Buy: Available online through various travel and tourism websites, as well as at major tourist information centers in Athens.

Website: Athens City Pass

Athens Sightseeing Pass

Overview: This pass provides access to a selection of Athens' top attractions, with options for different durations.

Features:

1, 2, or 3-Day Pass: Allows entry to a list of selected sites, including the Acropolis, the National Archaeological Museum, and the Temple of Olympian Zeus. The multi-day options often provide unlimited access over the chosen period.

Additional Discounts: Includes discounts on guided tours and dining options.

Where to Buy: Purchase online in advance or at tourist information centers.

Website: Athens Sightseeing Pass

Athens Acropolis Pass

Overview: Specifically focused on the Acropolis and its related sites, this pass is ideal for visitors who want to explore the Acropolis complex thoroughly.

Features:

Single or Multi-Day Pass: Offers entry to the Acropolis Museum and several other sites within the Acropolis area, including the Parthenon and the Odeon of Herodes Atticus.

Skip-the-Line Access: Often includes skip-the-line privileges, saving time during peak tourist periods.

Where to Buy: Available online, at the Acropolis entrance, and at various authorized ticket sellers.

Website: Acropolis Pass

Athens Combo Pass

Overview: Combines entry to multiple attractions, offering a convenient and cost-effective option for those planning to visit several sites.

Features:

Combination Tickets: Includes access to major sites such as the Acropolis, the Ancient Agora, the Roman Agora, and the Temple of Olympian Zeus.

Discounted Rates: Often provides a discount compared to purchasing individual tickets for each attraction.

Where to Buy: Purchase online or at major tourist information centers.

Website: Athens Combo Pass

Athens Transport Pass

Overview: Although not a tourist pass for attractions, the Athens Transport Pass is valuable for visitors using public transportation.

Features:

1, 3, or 7-Day Pass: Provides unlimited travel on Athens' metro, buses, and trams.

Airport Transfers: Some versions include airport transfers, making it convenient for arrivals and departures.

Where to Buy: Available at metro stations, kiosks, and online.

Website: Athens Transport Pass

These passes can streamline your sightseeing experience, offering both convenience and potential savings. Be sure to choose the one that best fits your itinerary and interests.

Printed in Great Britain
by Amazon

58101569R10109